PRAISE FOR PAG⟨

"This book is full of magickal pr⟨
and affordable…It offers a grou⟨
experiences and limitations of p⟨
experiences when we are in limite⟨ ⟩ ⟨ ⟩ ⟨t as an essential
resource to fill the gap between living a whole life or returning
to a life that leads back to incarceration. I, also, recommend this
book to young readers interested in Paganism who might be on a
destructive path. I believe that it would help them to wake up and
recognize how to walk in the world, be grateful for the freedom
that they currently have, and move them away from possibly entering the system…Whether you are an individual on parole, a family
member, anyone within the criminal justice system, or a curious
mind, this is a practical guide on how to approach life with respect,
how to approach self-care, and how to be a happy, successful person at any point in your path."

—Granddaughter Crow, author of *Belief,
Being, and Beyond*

"Awyn Dawn continues her quest to advise the formerly incarcerated Pagan community on how to navigate the transition from
behind the concrete to parolee. Her charming mix of magical
instruction and blunt reality is refreshing and needed. She offers
her lived experience in both spiritual paths and everyday living. I
recommend this book to anyone who lives or works in this space."

—JoyBelle Phelan, program assistant for the
University of Denver Prison Arts Initiative
(DU PAI) and Prison Journalism Project

"Awyn Dawn has done it again! Her ability to share her life with us through Paganism, intuition, and practical spells is not just for parolees, but for the everyday person wanting to open their minds and abilities! She provides us with the basics and takes us beyond, allowing us to go as far as we want in a clear and precise way. A must have for every Pagan's shelf!"

—Melanie Barnum, author of *Intuition at Work*

PAGANISM
on
PAROLE

ABOUT THE AUTHOR

Awyn Dawn is a Pagan high priestess who has been working with spiritual seekers for nearly ten years. After being incarcerated and overcoming her own life challenges, Awyn dedicated herself to the Pagan path and now teaches others in the Colorado prison system. Awyn is Reiki II-attuned and has a BS in Integrative Health Care from MSU-Denver. She is a member of the Society of Authors and the International Women's Writing Guild.

Alin,
May all your
words be magic!

Awyn

PAGANISM
on
PAROLE

Connecting to the Magic All Around

Author of *Paganism for Prisoners*

AWYN DAWN

Llewellyn Publications
Woodbury, Minnesota

FIRST EDITION
First Printing, 2022

Book layout by Mandie Brasington
Cover design by Kevin R. Brown
Interior art by the Llewellyn Art Department

Llewellyn Publications is a registered trademark of Llewellyn Worldwide Ltd.

Library of Congress Cataloging-in-Publication Data (Pending)
ISBN: 978-0-7387-6993-6

Llewellyn Publications
A Division of Llewellyn Worldwide Ltd.
2143 Wooddale Drive
Woodbury, MN 55125-2989
www.llewellyn.com

Printed in the United States of America

OTHER BOOKS BY AWYN DAWN

Paganism for Prisoners: Connecting to the Magic Within

I dedicate this book to all those who,
despite having a messy past, still hold on to the hope
that life can be different.

To Aaron, Michelle, and JoyBelle
for being an integral part of my own growth.
Without the seeds you planted and the support you have given,
this would not be possible.

And my dear Penelope, *never* forget the haberdashery!

CONTENTS

RITUALS, MEDITATIONS, AND EXERCISES

DISCLAIMER

Common sense is a virtue, one which you should utilize at every given opportunity. The words expressed in this book are based off my experiences. If there is a suggestion I provide that will get you in trouble while on parole, then don't do it. This book is only a guide. Remember, we are each responsible for our own choices. Nothing in this book is an order. Even if direction and instruction is provided, it is up to you to determine if you can and should do it.

FOREWORD

By Dodie Graham McKay

When I first began my journey into Witchcraft and Paganism, I was a teenager, and it was the late 1980s. There were open circles to attend, bookstores with occult sections, and a couple of teachers offering classes in Witchcraft. As time went by and I attended more publicly offered events, the phrase that I kept hearing was "building community." In those days, the most common way for someone interested in Witchcraft and Paganism to find like-minded individuals to learn from and practice with was to go to a "community building" event and introduce themselves to folks and see what happened.

Well, it worked. Community was built. Flash forward to the present day and Paganism and Witchcraft traditions are growing in popularity and are being embraced by a wider and more diverse circle of people than ever before. So now that we have the numbers, what can we offer these folks? Do the modern Pagan and Witchcraft communities offer warm welcomes, access and resources to all seekers? For a community to thrive, we need more than just numbers; we need something more substantial, we need something to feed and nourish this community. We need culture.

Culture is the way a community shares its art, language, knowledge, beliefs, rules, and way of life. Culture is a shared way of expressing attitudes, social practices and behaviors that are passed down through generations. We are living at a point in history where the modern Pagan and Witchcraft movements are young enough that we can all actively participate in shaping a contemporary culture for our traditions that is fair and inclusive, a culture that celebrates everyone.

Over the last forty or so years, pagan and Witchcraft groups have worked to build cultural institutions that support many great causes. Pagan and Witchcraft writers, teachers and artists get tremendous support from our communities. Our work is purchased, shared, and celebrated in many forums. Pagan organizers have worked hard to create festivals and Pagan pride events that showcase the talented speakers and presenters who represent our traditions. Some of these folks enjoy a sort of celebrity status and acclaim within these circles.

We have seen Pagan leaders and interfaith groups work towards our traditions gaining recognition as viable churches and as an acceptable religious or spiritual alternative. We have seen the fight for the pentacle as a symbol of faith in the armed forces. We have seen the creation of educational material for law enforcement so that they may differentiate between sincere Pagans and actual problematic offenders. These victories celebrate and support our Pagan and Witchcraft heroes, but what about our underdogs? Are marginalized folks in our communities being celebrated and supported as much as our heroes?

Many of us who come to Pagan and Witchcraft spaces are here because in some way we are outside of the norms of mainstream society. Our spiritual beliefs just do not conform, and maybe other aspects of our lives are outside the box as well, and we feel that within Pagan and Witchcraft communities we will be accepted and valued for the individuals that we are. If other folk living on the edge of mainstream society—like a Pagan or Witch recently released from prison—can't find community with other Pagans and Witches, where can they find it? This brings me back to that culture thing, and the opportunity we have to build an inclusive one.

When I learned about the publication of Awyn Dawn's first book, *Paganism for Prisoners: Connecting to the Magic Within*, I was blown away. It put a huge smile on my face to learn that a large commercial publisher was taking a chance and releasing a book for incarcerated Pagans written by a formerly incarcerated Pagan high priestess! I could see that this segment of the Pagan population was being valued and that content was being created to serve them. This is community service, and it is building our collective culture. We are growing up into a community that really is building attitudes, social practices and behavior that supports the growth and practice of Pagans and Witches in prison. And then it got better. A second book!

Out of the blue, I received an email from my editor at Llewellyn that Awyn Dawn was interested in connecting with me. I sent her a note to say hi, and received an email back asking if I would be willing to write the foreword to her follow up book, *Pagans on Parole*. She sent me a copy of her manuscript and I quickly realized how valuable a resource it is for those of us who work in magic circles, covens, groves, training groups, classes or kindreds with folks who have been in prison and are in the process of building new lives, magical practices and spirituality. It provided me with insight on the unique challenges that are faced by someone standing in that place between incarceration and freedom. It helped me understand how to be of better service and support to folks who are often overlooked and underestimated.

If you are currently incarcerated or on parole, the book you hold in your hands is a handbook for you as you transition out of prison and into a world of unknown challenges. Your guide, Awyn Dawn, has taken these steps and accepted those challenges. Her suggestions and advice are no-nonsense and straight from the heart. By following them, you will find yourself on the road to finding a place within the Pagan and Witchcraft community. Her exercises, spells, rituals, and practical magic provide an easy-to-understand framework for a satisfying magical practice.

When I see this book, along with *Paganism for Prisoners*, on bookstore shelves and popping up in my social media feed, I think it sends a message to incarcerated folks and parolees, that we, the wider Pagan and Witchcraft communities, see you and we support you. We are lifting each other up, and we are creating a more inclusive and accessible culture for everyone.

INTRODUCTION

If you have just been released from jail or prison, congratulations! I mean it, congratulations. You are at a crossroads, one of many that happens in life. For centuries, the importance of crossroads has been noted in the lore and legends of goddesses, such as the Greek Hecate. Crossroads, whether real or symbolic, mark a time of possibility, a place that exists between the worlds. You are now at a point in your life where you are at a crossroads, no longer an inmate, but not yet free. The choices you make over the length of your parole/probation will determine if you increase your freedom or if you go back to your "three hots and a cot." Make no mistake, you do have a choice in the matter.

It was many years ago when I first knew that I was Pagan. When I was in prison, I renewed my spirituality. But it was during the time I spent on parole that I started to really put in the work. I found a group on Meetup.com and started to attend classes. I never missed one. In just over a year, I was initiated. A few years later, around the time I started taking a course into the prison system, I got my second-degree initiation. Then a few years after that, I became a high priestess. None of this would have happened if I had sat idly by and waited for the gods to come knock on my door. I had to seek them out. Once I did, I found that they were not difficult to find. They simply wanted me to show them what I was willing to put into my spiritual path, then boom, they were as easy to find as a leaf on the ground in autumn.

Do not interpret this to mean that once you walk a path that feeds your spirit your life will be an easy one. What I have found is that the support I get from the gods provides me with the ability to constantly step through challenges. Each of these challenges became like a rung on a ladder, helping me climb higher and higher. There is an ability to thrive despite hardships that comes from living a life full of said hardships. What often becomes the biggest challenge to those on parole is not the adversity that is faced but the failure to believe that a better future awaits. If you choose to walk forward, despite fear, reservations, and the comfort of the familiar, you will be amazed by what you can achieve.

As you read the following chapters, know that it is wisdom gained from personal experience that is being imparted. I did something different when I got out of prison. I did whatever I needed to do to not go back. That meant changing many things. Most things. Everything. But the freedom I now possess is greater than anything that I ever hoped to have when I was out running the streets and "doing the most." Some of what you read in here will be things you do not want to hear or maybe are just not ready to hear. The discomfort of these parts is necessary. Change does not happen in the comfort zone. If you want to change, there is going to be some discomfort. The more willing you are to accept this, the less difficult the process can be.

It is not my goal to force you, kicking and screaming, into change. If we are being honest, you know the road that takes you back to prison; You know it quite well. What you likely do not know is the path that leads to life, to truly living. You may not feel worthy of this second option, or you may feel like it is not something you can acquire, but these ideas are incorrect. If you can say to yourself "Maybe, just maybe, there is something better in store for me than being locked up," then I encourage you to take the next steps. This book is not the end-all-be-all of things you need to know. But it is full of magical ideas that kept me from being a recidivism statistic. If they worked for me, they could work for you too.

One of the most beautiful things I learned as I went through all the hoops that parole requires was how to integrate my spiritual practice in my everyday life. I am not only a priestess on Saturdays or when ritual is happening. Instead, I strive to live my life in a way that honors the gods. Walking my spiritual path, as opposed to just focusing on the surface, is what has allowed me to go from a drug addict with felonies to a college graduate, author, energy healer, and a kind and compassionate—though far from perfect—human being.

This book, *Paganism on Parole*, is the follow-up to *Paganism for Prisoners: Connecting to the Magic Within*. As such, I have gone to great lengths to present different information whenever possible. The core foundations of change though will inevitably have some overlap. That's okay. If you are anything like me, you sometimes need to hear things more than once before they set in. Be patient with yourself, even if you do not learn everything all at once. Really, in the simplest way, all you must do is just try to be a little better than you were yesterday and forgive yourself when you are not.

Remember, for now, that you are almost free. *Almost* free. Not yet. It is much harder to earn your freedom when you have a taste of it than when you have no taste of it at all. It is easier to do the things you are supposed to when there are guards and surveillance cameras to force you into accountability. Soon, if not already, you will not have these things. So, you must be accountable to yourself, honest with yourself, and true to yourself. This is where your power lies, not in any spell nor tool, but in the awareness of self that you gain by walking a path with the gods. It is the freedom found here that can never be stripped away, unless you let it.

However, power comes with great responsibility. Having the power to make decisions does not free you from the consequences of those decisions. In fact, I have found that power means I have greater accountability for my actions. I no longer get the luxury of using "I didn't know" as an excuse. I do know better. At first the awareness that you know better may fill you with anxiety. Most of you reading this will have experiences in your past that are neither comfortable nor pretty. You're not alone. For now, wake up each morning, take a deep breath, and know that the gods, in any of their many forms, are with you. They will let you make mistakes to learn lessons, but they will also bestow guidance and wisdom for those who seek it.

Go forward!

CHAPTER 1
COMMUNITY

Community, connection, and belonging; human beings are social creatures. With very few exceptions, we do not do well in isolation. After a while people may adapt to isolation but this is not where people thrive. The first villages to exist did so to establish community. Back then, community meant safety and genetic diversity. It meant that there were others to share stories with and to jointly share in the labor. It meant sharing happiness and sharing grief. It meant connection. This connection to others allowed humanity to develop a strength that could not be gained on its own. Communities even helped—and continue to—shape our identities. The tribe, village, area, or region a person came from could indicate what language they were likely to speak, what clothing they were likely to use, and even certain mannerisms.

Today, this drive to belong still exists within us. For some of us, the urge is so strong that we would rather put ourselves in harm's way than to give up the only sense of community we have ever known. Community connections can feel so strong that we fear if we lose them, we will lose all sense of self-identity.

As you read through this chapter, remember that I am not trying to tell you who to spend time with. That is a decision which is wholly yours. I will say, though, that adding supportive people to your connections can make a difference between making choices that lead you back to prison or choices that keep you out of it. If you already have a good support system, this chapter can help you add to it. If you, like so many, do not have healthy connections, then what do you have to lose by trying to develop some?

HOW TO FIND A PAGAN COMMUNITY

Where does a person even begin to look for supportive people to hang around? What do supportive people do? How do they act? How do you find them? To begin answering these questions, think about unsupportive people. We have all encountered them. These are people who always have reasons why you can't better your life. Or those who only call when they need a favor. Or who talk you into doing things that are dangerous, illegal, or you are simply not comfortable with. They can also be people who sign off on all your bad decisions.

People who are supportive may provide constructive criticism but want to see you succeed. Healthy people are not afraid to say no and respect when you say no. There may be some trial and error while you look for people who are supportive, but beginning to identify who you are as a person can help direct you to the people you resonate with. You may have worn many masks in the past to try to fit in with a person or group and gain their acceptance. This is the time to strip away those masks and really be you.

Online

Depending on how long you have been incarcerated, using the internet may or may not be a challenge. Regardless of your personal comfort level, it is a great resource for finding Pagan groups and events in your area. If you are new to the internet, that is okay. I have included offline methods for finding events later in the chapter. I would still encourage you to get the assistance of a friend, family member, or even ask a librarian to give you some pointers for navigating the digital world we now live in.

Social Media

There are literally thousands of groups you can find on social media. On Facebook, for example, you can find groups for Heathens, Druids, Pagans, Witches, Wiccans, often grouped by region or flavor by which the group practices. It is up to you to use common sense when filtering through these groups. Almost without exception, those who scream the loudest aren't actually saying anything. Groups that require large sums of money, sexual favors, illegal behaviors to join, or claim to have "the right way" are sketchy to say the least. You can do better, trust me.

The rest comes down to what you are looking for. Are you looking for a group with experienced members? Or people with your same skill level? Perhaps you want to find a group that holds online sabbats? There is a group for almost anything on the different social media platforms. Once again, I will advise you to use common sense. But, other than that, it can be a great starting point, especially if you are new to Paganism.

Websites and Apps

The first working Pagan group I ever joined was one I found through a website I happened across while just looking for activities to do in my area. There are websites and apps specifically designed to help people find events to attend and activities to participate in. Sometimes you must get a little creative. Yes, you may find groups that are outwardly Pagan. However, do not despair if the search proves difficult. Look for other common interests such as archery groups, medieval reenactors, workshops that relate to alternative spirituality, Pagan author book signings, a local area Pagan Pride Day, seminars, and other activities. Look for the things you are interested in and ask the gods to bring you those who can help you to move forward on your spiritual path.

Online groups often give you a chance to get a feel for what a group is like. Talk to members, see what kind of events they have (if any), and make sure that their moral compass aligns with yours. Many online groups even offer streams to classes and rituals. As with all other things in life, use common sense. While meeting new people provides a certain level of security, never dismiss your intuition. If you feel like you shouldn't participate, don't. And while we're talking about safety, know that just because a group claims to be Pagan does not mean you have to settle for the first group you find. This goes for both online and in person groups.

Some other websites you can try are thetroth.org, facebook .com/TheWitchesVoiceInc, cog.org, druidry.org, wicpagtimes .com, and hellenicfaith.com, each of which has a slightly different focus. If you have any authors that you like, follow their social media; sometimes they host workshops and events that can be a good way to find like-minded individuals.

Digital Magazines

While you can still attain hard copies of many magazines, there is an increasing number of magazines available online. What's great about e-zines, aside from their eco-consciousness, is that a greater diversity can come through. Magazines are expensive to print and send out. Electronic versions still have overhead but it is considerably less. What this means for the reader (that's you) is that magazines that are more specific are more readily available. The ads and articles found in them can provide a great resource to events taking place in your area. Some good ones to start with are *Witches and Pagans, Pagan Dawn, PanGaia, Celtic Nations, Witch Way,* and *Sage Woman* magazine.

Blogs

Blogs are useful for many reasons. You can find out information, often ask questions, and depending on the blog you find, there may be links to upcoming events in your area. I encourage you to investigate a few of them and see which blog or blogs seem to be your flavor and suit your need.

In Person

My favorite communities are all in person. While online is great, there is something very different about sitting with a group of friends, or one close friend, and talking about the gods, the nature of the universe, life, food, frivolity, anything and nothing. The best part is doing this while phones are put away and the crescent moonlight fails to reveal the hours which have passed. Online mediums can open a door to in person events, but you are still more likely to find in person groups if you go to places in person and ask around.

DOC Volunteers

Was there a temple, coven, or Pagan-affiliated group that volunteered in the prison when you were incarcerated? Or one that sent in resources? Now that you are out, find out if they have a website or social media account and use appropriate channels to see if they can refer you to some local groups or if they know about some upcoming events. While DOC rules might not permit them to train you or build friendships while you are on paper, they likely know the community and can point you in the right direction.

Community Buildings / Campuses

Community center buildings, whether in town or on campuses, usually have bulletin boards where people and organizations can post events. The same holds true for college campuses. Larger campuses tend to have more postings. There are even virtual bulletin boards you can find on some of their websites.

Bookstores

It seems so obvious but bookstores, particularly the new age, occult, and metaphysical bookstores are usually run by people who are either in the Pagan community or those who know people who are. There is no harm in introducing yourself, saying you are new to the community, and would like to know how to find local Pagan groups. You can even ask around for Heathen groups, Druidic groups, eclectic groups, those who practice with Mesopotamian deities, Ancient Egyptian deities, Hellenic deities, or anything that interests you. The bonus is that these stores have books. That alone is worth the trip.

Unitarian Universalist Churches

Do not be put off by the word church. Unitarian Universalist are very open, generally speaking, and they even have the Covenant of Unitarian Universalist Pagans (CUUPs). There are many Witches, Wiccans, and Pagans that join a CUUPs chapter and find a strong sense of community there.

Events / Festivals

Throughout the country, there are festivals and events such as Pagan Pride Day, public sabbat or esbat gatherings, dragon festivals, renaissance fairs, days to honor specific deities, craft fairs, vendor markets, feast days, and more. A simple online search for

"Pagan festivals" will bring up everything from metaphysical fairs to dances and everything in between.

If you are going to an event, don't forget to get your parole officer's permission, especially if traveling or if you'll be out past curfew. Once there you can talk to people, attend workshops, and ask around for groups that are open to new members. Events are also a great place to look for magical items such as tools, herbs, decorations, and jewelry.

Another advantage to attending festivals is that they are fun and give you a chance to escape the mundane world, if only for a bit. Many are even family friendly, making them a place where you can spend time with your kids while still connecting to new friends. The family-friendly events tend to have a stricter alcohol and substance use policy. If you have had issues with these, then going to the family-friendly events may be something to consider as a starting point.

Start One

For whatever reason, if you are not able to find community in your area, start a group. Go with whatever your comfort level is. Maybe you start a Pagan book club or invite a few friends to dance under a full moon. If you can lead a ritual, that's great. If you are not there yet, that's okay too. Starting a group of any kind is like sending out a beacon for other seekers. You can still practice as a solitary if you want to but working in a close-knit group does have certain advantages, such as having someone to bounce ideas off.

NON-PAGAN COMMUNITY

Supportive people do not have to be just in your spiritual community, they can be found in other communities as well. Ask yourself what you like to do. What are your hobbies and interests? It has probably been a very long time since you have asked yourself these questions. Take your time and think about it. In the meantime, let's look at some of the activities and groups that can stem from your answers.

Hobbies

It may be a hard task at first to determine what you like to do for fun. For some of you reading this, it may have a long time since you've asked yourself the question "What do I enjoy?" Having hobbies serves a few different purposes. It gives you something productive to do with your time, brings you joy (why bother having a hobby you don't like), and introduces you to a new group of people who share your interests.

The bulletin boards and other places mentioned earlier are a good way to find hobbies. This is a good way to be adventurous. If it doesn't interfere with the conditions of your parole, why not take that painting class, learn to make pottery, go LARPing (live action role playing), or try out rock climbing? You are being given a second chance (or sometimes a third or fourth). I challenge you to try something you have never given yourself permission to try before. If you don't like it, at least you know that for sure.

Sports/Athletics

Much of what has already been said about hobbies applies to sports as well. Being on a team or having a workout buddy helps create accountability. A person is more likely to wake up to go for a run if they have a friend counting on them. Look in some of the previously mentioned locations for softball teams, flag football, bowling leagues, or anything as long as it gets you up and moving. If you, like me, are not particularly coordinated, there are still options: hiking, walking, jogging, tai chi, yoga, spin class, etc.

Get creative and be open. Something you never considered may be your next passion.

Recovery and Twelve Step

Not all of you reading this will need to worry about this section. But considering that 20 percent of the incarcerated population is in for drug related offenses, I am willing to bet that many of you should take an extra moment here.[1] Substance use treatment may or may not be one of your parole requirements. Either way, if you have even an inkling that you should check out an addiction recovery support meeting, then please do. There are meetings online and in person for just about everything. Some of the most well-known are twelve-step based and include Alcoholics Anonymous (AA), Narcotics Anonymous (NA), Crystal Meth Anonymous (CMA), Cocaine Anonymous (CA) and Co-Dependents Anonymous (CoDA). There are some other variations, many of which don't use a twelve step model, these include Advocates for Recovery (AFR), Pagans in Recovery, Recovery Dharma, and SMART recovery. These are great ways to find recovery outside of treatment centers. Each has its own personality, so it is up to you to decide which to try and which, if any, feel like home. More information can be found in the resources section at the end of the book.

Support Groups

Getting help is not a sign of weakness. It is a huge strength to be able to admit that we can't conquer the world alone. It is common for people who have been in jails or prisons to have trauma in their

1. Wendy Sawyer and Peter Wagner, "Mass Incarceration: The Whole Pie 2020," Mass Incarceration: The Whole Pie 2020 | Prison Policy Initiative, March 24, 2020, https://www.prisonpolicy.org/reports/pie2020.html.

past, frequently in childhood and adolescence. I guarantee you are not alone. Some of the groups you might consider looking into are Help for Adult Victims of Child Abuse (HAVOCA), Adult Survivors of Child Abuse (ASCA), the WINGS Foundation (childhood sexual abuse support), National Association of Adult Survivors of Child Abuse (NAASCA), The Blue Bench (sexual assault survivors), PTSD Alliance, and Emotions Anonymous (emotional support). PsychologyToday.com and SAMHSA.gov have additional support resources for many different types of people, including support groups specifically for men and young adults, who are statistically less likely to seek out support than other groups. The Department of Veteran's Affairs has specific resources for PTSD. More information on these and other organizations can be found in the resources section of this book.

DISCUSSING INCARCERATION

It is up to you to choose to reveal that you were recently released from prison. It is a judgment call and one that I cannot make for you. But I can present both sides of the argument to help you decide what you feel is most appropriate for your situation. Being able to make your own decisions and deal with the consequences thereof is one of the greatest freedoms you have. Informed decisions frequently mean the difference between having consequences thrust upon us and being prepared to face them.

Even in the Pagan communities, not everyone understands the various socioeconomic, personal, and other factors that frequently contribute to incarceration. However, my experience in Pagan communities has been that there are more open-minded people than not. This is likely to depend on where you live though. If you tell someone or a group that you are recently released from prison, they could embrace you, they could despise you, or they could reserve judgment and base their decision on who you are as a human being. You have no control over their response. Scary as it is to not have control, sometimes it is an act of faith.

If you don't tell them, well, secrets like this usually come out in the wash. Once again, their response is outside of your control. One option you have is to do neither. Don't make it the first thing you say about yourself nor lie about it if it comes up. Another option is to tell the high priest/ess (or the group leader) privately and ask them how you should proceed. If they have been leading the group for a while, they likely know the personalities in the group. Ultimately, remember that if you get asked to leave a group, it is not the group for you. Respect their wishes and leave with dignity. You can yell and scream about it in private later, but leave with honor.

WHAT ABOUT OLD FRIENDS AND FAMILY?

I want to start this section by telling you something that I think everybody should know regardless of how long you have a known a person or what you have been through together: not everyone is worth keeping in your life. This is a hard lesson, I know, but you are doing something different. You are making a choice to avoid another sentence and will, instead, point your life down a path where you can walk with the gods and have your head held high. The people who are worth keeping in your life will make themselves known, through action and through deed. Some of the relationships you had before going to prison can be salvaged, others cannot. Some relationships aren't worth trying to salvage. Let the wreckage of the latter serve as reminders of what life doesn't have to be.

Oh, but wait, this is not a one-way street. Most of you, I would venture to say all of you, will have caused damage through your past actions. Did incarceration cost your family monetary support? Maybe they had to move, or they no longer talk to you because they are embarrassed by what you did. Did you steal from them? Lie to them? Make empty promises? I don't bring this up to make you feel bad. I just know that when I got out of prison, I had a long list of horrible things I had done to people. If you want to rebuild relationships, you also must try to be the kind of person people want to rebuild relationships with.

The Broom Closet

One of the first questions you may be asking is do I tell my friends and family that I'm Pagan? If so, how? I cannot answer the first question for you. Everyone has different reasons for staying in the broom closet or for being open about their faith. You may choose to let friends know but not family or vice versa. Today it seems like people, generally speaking, are more open-minded than they were in the past. This doesn't mean that all people are open-minded. You know your family much better than I do, so meditate and pray and, ultimately, go with your instinct. Sometimes the reactions people have may surprise you. Even a person who is adamantly opposed to your Paganism at first may eventually come around. Or they may not. Like I said, this is an incredibly personal choice. If you do decide to let people know, I have included some tips in the next section that are generally helpful for this kind of thing.

How to Tell Them

In this section, I want to start off by saying that you do not have to feel bad or guilty or embarrassed by your faith. I really hope that this is not how being Pagan makes you feel. It should be empowering and affirming and comfortable. The reason this is being said is because many of you may come from very religiously dogmatic families. If you decide to tell certain family members, remember that you are NOT issuing an apology. You may have things to apologize to them for, but your faith is not one of them. You are instead welcoming them to know another side of you that may have been hidden previously. You are honoring them with the knowledge.

Which People

First, decide who you are going to tell. There tend to be two basic reactions that new Pagans will have. The first reaction may be that a new Pagan is frightened to tell people, afraid of the reaction they will recieve, or feel unprepared to answer the questions they may be asked. The second reaction may be that they get so excited that they want to tell everyone. Personally, I think your selection process should be somewhere in the middle. Does your boss need to know? No, it is not their business. Does your mom? This one is a little harder to answer. Hopefully, you have a supportive mom who loves you for you. In this case, it really comes down to how you feel about it. Each person should be decided on in a case-by-case basis. I wear my pentacle with pride and am very out of the broom closet. This still doesn't mean that I introduce myself with "Hi, I'm Awyn. I'm a Witch." Faith is personal and sacred. Who you tell should reflect that.

Timing

When you choose to tell friends, family, or acquaintances is as important as whether to tell them in the first place. There is a lot of common sense that goes with this. If your uncle just got devastating news, pick another time. You can time when you tell them to days of week, then use items, colors, and numbers associated with that day to help you.

- *Sunday:* The day of the sun. This is a good day to utilize self-expression, friendliness, and warm feelings. Sunday also represents the paternal connection, so if you are looking for a day to tell your dad, Sunday may be a good choice. You can carry a piece of tiger's eye or carnelian with you and burn a gold, yellow, or orange candle to aid you.

- *Monday:* The day of the moon. Monday is a day for healing, family, and family healing. Maternal connection is emphasized on this day, it is a good time to tell mom. For stones, carry moonstone, clear quartz, or a sapphire. Burn a white, pale blue, or silver candle.

- *Wednesday:* This is Wodin's (Odin's) day. Wednesday is one of the best days for communication and brings insight with it. On this day, carry a set of lodestones, agate, or turquoise with you. Burn a purple, orange, or yellow candle.

- *Friday:* This is Freyja or Frigg's day. This is a good day to tell anyone you are romantically or sexually involved with or anyone you have given life to (your kids). Carry a piece of alexandrite, amber, or rose quartz and burn a pink or aqua candle.

One-on-One versus a Group

There are definite pros and cons when it comes to discussing you sprituality in either a one-on-one setting or in a group setting. On the one hand, if you tell multiple family members at once, you don't have to make the initial announcement as many times. However you may find yourself bombarded by questions from multiple family members. If you tell them each one by one, you do have make the initial announcement more frequently but you can personalize the setting in which you tell them.

What if they ask you questions? You can answer them the best you are able, say you don't know the answer, or tell them you are not comfortable with the question. Just because this is your faith does not mean you have to be able to answer any questioned posed to you. You can simply say, "You know, that is a good question. I'm not sure of the answer myself, but I'm excited to find out," or "I don't want to answer that question."

Ask for Their Time

This doesn't have to be something big and formal. However, you are about to tell someone something they may or may not respond well to, so it is a courtesy to ask them if they have a few moments for you to talk to them. This will give them the subconscious message that you are about to discuss something important with them and it gives them the opportunity to decline. If they say that it is not a good time, then ask them when they would be available.

Be Confident

You are doing this person the courtesy of letting them know that you're Pagan. The way they react is something you have no control over. However, the way you react to their reaction is in your control. It might be helpful to have some blanket phrases to say for some possible outcomes such as "Thank you for being so supportive. I was nervous to tell you," or "I can see this is upsetting you. How about we step away from this topic, and when you have had some time to process it, I would be willing to answer some of your questions." These responses can give you an out and keep the situation from turning unpleasant.

Then What?

Well, that is largely up to you. From personal experience, I can tell you that once you make it known to your friends that you read cards or know spell craft, you will get asked to do these things for people. Most of the time the people who ask are trying to be supportive and excited for you. But, and this is a big but, you are not obligated to say yes. Reading cards takes a lot of energy, especially if you are channeling the answers. If you start doing this for all your friends, family, acquaintances, and anyone else who asks, you can get burned out. There is an energetic exchange that should be kept, a give and take instead of a take, take, take, or give, give, give.

It will serve you well to consider not making these things widely known unless you have the boundaries to either say no or to insist on energetic exchange (payment, trade, etc.) for your services. Social media is full of people who will announce that they will read for anyone who responds to a post. While this isn't necessarily bad or wrong, remember that people will line up for something that is free and not always value it.

Religious Family Functions

Whether you choose to remain in the broom closet or swing the door open for the world to see, there will likely be family functions in your future. How do you celebrate sabbats and spend time with your family for the holidays? Luckily, there are a lot of solutions. You just have to pick the one that makes the most sense for your situation.

The first option is to celebrate both. Let's look at the winter solstice, Yule. It falls a few days before Christmas. You can celebrate Yule, then go join your family for Christmas traditions. I can't speak for the gods but I have never had one get mad at me for enjoying life and spending time with my family. With this option, you can join your family's religious holiday after any of their religious services are over. If your family goes to church from ten to eleven in the morning, show up at 11:30 or just tell them you want to spend time with them but have no interest going to the religious part.

The next option is to merge your Pagan holiday traditions with your family's spiritual traditions. Once again, let's look at Yule. Trees, lights, apple cider, laughter, merriment, these are all standard in both Yule and Christmas. Want to open a gift on Yule? Go ahead. If you want to decorate eggs on Ostara and again on Easter, do it. You do not have to avoid your family around the holidays just because you are Pagan.

You can also consider inviting your family to take part in Ostara, Yule, or Midsummer with you. If your family is open-minded enough to want to see what your celebrations look like, this is an incredible thing. The point of all of this is that you don't have to make holidays harder than they must be. I know many Pagans who celebrate Yule and its traditions, then open gifts on December 25. If you want to boycott non-Pagan holidays, you can. You are certainly allowed to, but it is not a requirement of Paganism.

Regaining Trust

We're going to switch gears for a moment and talk about what happens if your family isn't ready to welcome you back. If this is the case, know that you are not alone. I am not here to assign blame or to analyze who did what to who. It's not my business. What I am here to do is to help guide you to be able to make your own responsible decisions. You'd be surprised how much effect just living a good life can on other people's willingness to forgive and forget the past. However, you can't make anybody get to that point. What you can do is work on making who you are into someone who is trustworthy. You do this by incorporating all the things mentioned already in this book. Remember that actions speak louder than words. How many times have you promised not to do something only to do it again a mere week later? When you let your actions speak, they will not be filled with empty promises. Instead, those actions will illustrate the traits that live in your soul.

WHAT IF MY FAMILY IS TOXIC?

Toxic families are a real thing. If you have a family that is full of people who cause you harm, belittle you, use you, or are unsupportive, it is okay to distance yourself from them. Nine times out of ten these are behaviors that have been passed down from one family member to another for many generations (generational trauma). If you recognize these behaviors, it means you have the chance to break the cycle of trauma. I wish I could tell you this process is fun and easy, but it takes work and sometimes hurts. It is absolutely worth the investment though. It is bittersweet to be the person in your bloodline who is responsible for healing it. However, it is a sacred duty.

There is a lot of time between the start of personal growth work and when you are far enough along in the process to ensure you won't pass on the generational trauma. What do you do in the meantime? One option is to distance yourself from your family. This can take many forms. It might mean only seeing them on holidays. It might mean only communicating via phone or giving yourself a time limit on talking to them. It could also include bringing a supportive friend to family gatherings. It may even include not seeing family at all for an indeterminate amount of time. It is okay to set these kinds of limits. You can always change them later. For now, you just must work on you.

Another option is to see if family members are willing to go to family/couples therapy with you. Having an unrelated person mediate a conversation is a great way to bypass the barriers of communication. Alternatively, the family members who are interested in therapy could go to individual counselors. Or both practices—group sessions and indiviual sessions—could be done. Mental wellness is undervalued in much of the world. But it really is a key piece to everything from spirituality to self-confidence. This is discussed in more detail in the mental health chapter, which is chapter two.

If you decide that being around your family is not healthy for you, this doesn't mean that you must be alone. Family doesn't have to mean someone who is biologically related. It can be anyone from your tribe, anyone who feels like family to you. Here is the catch though. We humans tend to surround ourselves with people who emulate what we have been taught or who fill a hole within us. Just be mindful that sometimes chosen family can be as toxic as regular family. Regardless of who makes up your family, you have a responsibility to each other to withhold healthy boundaries and interact in ways that respect one another.

SOUL MATES

Before we talk about soul mates, it's important to point out that you are a complete person all on your own! You are not missing a piece that can only be filled by another person. The reason to point this out is because it is all too common for people to justify staying in an abusive, controlling, or unhealthy relationship by saying that their abuser is a soul mate or twin flame. From this perspective, the idea of having a soul mate can be quite disempowering and dangerous.

More than that, this is not even what the term *soul mate* means. *Soul mate* does not necessarily mean a romantic partner, though it can. *Soul mate* can refer to another's soul self, with whom we have made an agreement to meet throughout incarnations and various roles. A person who is now your sibling may have been your parent or close friend in a past life. Soul mates are people who could also be teachers, guides, or many other types of roles. Some will stay in your life for a while, others may pop in and out, and still others may only be encountered once in this lifetime.

Also remember that even if that significant other you're dating is a soul mate, they may only be meant to make a cameo appearance in your life. Once you have learned the lessons you needed to learn from each other, or otherwise fulfilled your purpose, you are meant to part ways. Yes, it can be sad. But when we try to hang on to that which is no longer meant for us, there are outcomes and consequences. You will be blocking the next thing you are meant to receive from manifesting in your world.

SPELL TO ATTRACT FRIENDS

This spell is designed to help you find friends. It is not meant to make, coerce, or force a specific person to be your friend. Instead, it is more like a beacon, opening yourself up to allow friendship to enter your life.

What You Need

- A white or yellow candle. (A taper candle is preferred.)
- Candle holder.
- Matches.
- Oil that contains either daisy, lemon balm, passionflower, dandelion, or rose. If you don't know what oil to get, you

can always get some extra virgin olive oil and use it plain or mix it in with the crushed flowers of one of the plants listed.

- Optional: a piece of amber.

Steps

First, pick up your candle. Then, focus on the feeling you get when you meet someone new and it feels as though you have known them your whole life. Visualize this feeling filling up the candle and causing it to glow with a pastel soft yellow.

While still holding onto this feeling, anoint the candle (see chapter six on tolls and ritual items on how to anoint). Light the wick and say the following words three times:

> I call to me the friends I seek.
> I call to me the community I need.
> With support I will succeed.
> This is my will, so mote it be.

Let the candle burn down.

If you are using a piece of amber, leave it at the base of the candle holder until the candle is completely burned down. Carry the amber with you when you go to events where you are seeking to make new connections.

CORD-CUTTING SPELL

Everyone you meet leaves a little residual energy with you. Most of these smaller cords of energy will fizzle and dissipate with time. A cord-cutting spell can be used to remove these lesser cords of energy. It can also be used to remove bigger cords, such as cords left behind from a breakup. You may still feel that person's energetic ties for a while. A cord-cutting signifies that the relationship is over. A word of caution: do not perform this while the breakup is fresh. Allow the intensity of emotions that will initially flood you to dissipate so you can focus on the healing not on the hurt.

There are some larger cords that you will not want to remove. When you scan your body in the first part of the spell, you may notice the feeling of a large cord in the area just below your rib cage. This area is called the solar plexus. This is where familial and other important connections reside. You won't be cutting through this whole cord. But let's say you accidentally did cut through a cord for you parents, kids, or something similar. First of all, don't panic. Lifetime cords like this will reattach themselves. Try not to cut them, but don't panic if you do.

What You Need

- An item representing the person whose cord you are cutting.
- An athame. If you aren't allowed an athame due to probation restrictions, you may designate a butter knife or other similar item to serve as the cutting apparatus. It needn't be sharp to cut these cords on the astral plane.
- Two candles; one white and one black.
- Cord-cutting oil such as copal, sage, cedarwood, or your own specially-made blend.

Spell Part One: Removing Lesser Cords

This works best sky clad but can be done fully clothed. If you are wearing clothes, make sure they are loose and comfortable. Being barefoot helps you connect to the earth and is preferable for this kind of work.

Start off by getting in a relaxed and meditative state. This means you will want to focus on your breathing. Breathe in for a count of five, hold for three, breathe out for five. Do this until this breathing comes naturally.

With your eyes closed, you are going to mentally scan your skin. Start at your head and work your way down your body. What you're looking for are feelings of thin cords, much like the strands of a spider's web, attached to you at various points. Make note of where they are. You may notice some thicker cords; leave these alone for the moment and just focus on the thinner ones.

When you have scanned your whole body and found all these cords, it is time to remove them. Put a couple drops of cord-cutting oil on your athame and set it on the altar. Then, using both hands, grab the thin cords into bundles. These thin cords tend to attach in similar places, making them easy to bunch up into bundles. You might feel a grouping around your chest, arms, abdomen, and the like. One bundle at a time, grab the cords in one hand and your athame in the other. Cut through these cords. The cord-cutting oil should cause them to dissipate and disappear.

Once you have cut through all these bundles, dab a bit of the cord-cutting oil on the areas where the cords were removed, and say:

Cords removed shall not reattach.

These energies are gone; not even their memories last.

So shall it be.

Spell Part Two: Removing Larger Cords

Grab the item you've chosen to represent the person whose cords you will be cutting. Hold it in your hands, close your eyes, and focus on their energy. Now, scan your body and look for the place where it feels their cord is attached. If it is attached at your solar plexus, visualize pulling aside their strand and just cut the one, leaving the rest intact.

Anoint your athame on both sides with cord-cutting oil.

When you find their cord, hold it firmly in one hand. Think about a few definitive moments that cement your decision to cut the cord. When you feel that you have enough moments to cement your decision, hold the athame in your other hand and say:

> Distance and space is all that exists between us.
> There is nothing left to discuss.
> Our mission done. Time to part ways.
> That we may both be on to better things.

Cut the cord with your athame. See it turn to dust and vanish in your hand.Say, with conviction:

> Done, it's done, attached no more.
> Go in peace to never darken my door.

Rub some of the cord-cutting oil on the site of the cord removal. Wait a few days, then scan for the person's cords again using the item that represents them. If they are still attached, perform the ritual again. Keep rescanning every few days until the cords are gone. Once they are gone, destroy the item that represented them.

This last part is important, probably the most important piece: do not welcome them back. The cord will reattach and may be harder to get rid of next time. You've cut the cord. Don't stalk their social media, go to their work to see if they're there, send them texts, or any of these things. To cut the cord is to release them completely. If you keep them in your life, even if it's at the outskirts, you are undoing all the magic you just put in to cutting that cord.

CHAPTER 2
MENTAL HEALTH AND MAGIC

Being in jail or prison is an ordeal. It is an experience that cannot be understood in its entirety by those who have never been there. It changes you. But long before you were even locked up, the thoughts and behavior patterns you had been so used to had not been aligned with your highest self. This is the perfect time to realign your thoughts. I know you have a lot going on—UAs (urinalysis), meetings with your PO (parole officer), classes, and looking for a job. All this busyness is more reason to work on clearing and strengthening your mind. If your mind is strong, it is harder to be fooled, coerced, and manipulated. In addition to using magical and mystical means, do not ignore the importance of seeing a mental health professional. We all need someone to talk to sometimes.

By now you are probably thinking, *That's great, but how do I do that, Awyn?* Well, I would not simply say "Do this thing," without providing you ways to accomplish the task. As with most things, try different methods until you find what works. The beauty of Pagan paths, such as Wicca, Druidism, Heathenism, etc., is the ability to shape your world, your faith, your reality into whatever forms need to exist to help you resonate at your highest vibration. In layman's terms, if you like working with stones, do it. If you would rather use aromatherapy, do that. Now then, let's get into the how.

USING STONES FOR SUPPORT

Stones are amazing. They are easy to carry, can be carved, painted, added to magical pouches (sometimes called gris-gris bags), and used in dozens of other ways. For mental clarity and focus, there are some stones that are particularly potent. Your magical task can be to find, collect, buy, or trade some of these stones (whichever ones resonate with you) then make or buy a pouch to put them in and carry it with you. Each time you hold the pouch, know that it is promoting clarity in your mind.

Clear Quartz

Do not underestimate clear quartz based on its appearance. Due to it being colorless, it is limitless in its potential. It is associated with all the elements and all the zodiac signs. Clear quartz is a master at healing, with the ability to magnify mental energy, improve concentration, and increase memory. It is also great for neutralizing unwanted energy that can impact us mentally. This is especially true for people who are aware of their empathetic ability. This stone can be used to balance all the sides of yourself—mental, physical, emotional, and spiritual. It is also a great stone for channeling guardians, ancestors, and spirit guides.

Tiger's Eye

Perhaps it is my affinity for cats that is responsible for my love of tiger's eye. This stone helps you see. It helps you clearly see the paths that lie ahead. It helps you see situations accurately. Often our perspectives get clouded by emotions. Tiger's eye helps us see beyond the torrent of emotion and make a rational decision. It is called the stone of the mind because it promotes mental clarity and brings focus. It is also protective, helps with mood swings, and brings luck to the wearer.

Hematite

This reflective and magnetic stone has many purposes. Hematite may help stimulate blood flow through the body and decrease blood disorders. Similar to the other stones in this section, it is also a "stone for the mind"; specifically, hematite helps with mathematical and logical thought. It can also help you stay grounded in a room full of different energies.

Sodalite

Sodalite is often mistaken for lapis lazuli. The two have very similar properties and, magically speaking, sodalite can be substituted for lapis lazuli in most things. Sodalite is great for really connecting to your intuition, awakening your extrasensory senses, and enhancing your ability to observe the world around you. When you wear or carry sodalite, it stimulates your mind and helps you get the creative juices flowing. This stone serves to provide inspiration and help you get past creative roadblocks as well as promoting internal harmony.

Fluorite

Fluorite can help you focus on the goal at hand. If your mind is full of scattered thoughts, fluorite clears them away, allowing you to focus on one, the task at hand. It is also a good stone for clarification, especially if you are stuck in a situation where it feels as though you don't have all the information you need to make a wise decision. Fluorite comes in a variety of colors, from brown to blue to clear. The color you get comes down to intent and preference.

Since fluorite is an inexpensive stone, it is possible to have several shapes and varieties on hand.

Charoite

This purple stone aids you in putting your life into perspective and finding your place in the universe. Whether you need direction on the physical, mental, emotional, or spiritual level, charoite can help with healing and acceptance. It is a great stone to carry when you are trying to overcome fears because it will encourage you to face them. When you place it in your home, it helps protect your space and ensure your feelings of safety within it. If you have trouble sleeping at night, placing a piece of charoite in your pillowcase can help you ease into slumber.

AFFIRMATIONS

One magical practice I recommend everyone adopt is to write powerful statements or affirmations on your bathroom mirror with a dry erase marker. Every morning, even if you don't consciously see them, the affirmations written on your mirror will resonate within your subconscious mind and help change your conscious thoughts. If you can't do this for whatever reason, then put your affirmations someplace where you will see them every day and where nothing will be defaced in the process.

There are some guidelines for affirmations that will make them more powerful. The first of these is that it should be in the present tense: "I am," "I have," "I manifest." If you repeat to yourself "I will have strength," then you will find yourself in a constant state of thinking that someday you will have it, rather than having it now. Just like spell casting, when you put affirmations into the present, you are forcing them to manifest. On this same note, avoid words like *not*, *can't*, and *won't*. If you want your affirmation to be "I will not fail," then try making it "I will succeed." See how much more powerful and direct the second one is? Practice this with your own affirmations.

While you can find some great affirmations in books, and are certainly able to use prewritten ones, the ones you create yourself can be even stronger. You can customize your affirmations for your own purposes. These can be simple so they are easy to remember and can be recited anywhere. Words have power, so whenever possible, recite your affirmations aloud. Speaking your affirmations activates the left side of your brain, sends your words into the universe, and helps with manifestation.

Here are some simple examples:

- I am empowered to choose what is best for my life.
- I am the creator/creatrix of my own reality.
- I deserve wellness.
- The abundance of the universe flows within me.
- My possibilities are endless.
- I thrive!
- Prosperity is mine.
- My world, my rules.
- I have gratitude for _____.
- I am the sovereign of my own life.
- Good things come my way.

You get the idea. With each of the examples, there are positive reinforcements. Affirmations work so well because we are retraining the negative thought patterns that hold us back. When picking affirmations, start by thinking about your intention. What are the areas of your life that you want to improve? Do you have negative self-talk? Do you want to bring in more self-love? Are you trying to attract friends? Foster new life skills? The great thing about affirmations is that you can gear them toward any intention.

When you start a new affirmation—and yes you can do more than one—set a realistic expectation for how long, how often, and when you will say it. You might decide to say your affirmation every day with your morning coffee for two weeks. Then, if you want to continue, you might set the goal for another two weeks. This may be easier to stick to than a llonger length of time, such as six months.

YEARLY INTENTION

Something I like to do is to find a word that will serve as my intention for the year, then write a definition and an affirmation for it. For example, if you wanted to work on owning your power, you might choose the word *empowerment* or *empower*. Then you could write either the dictionary definition or write your own definition; a phrase such as "Self-actualized and true to self," could be an effective definition. An affirmation could then be created that reads "I own my power," or "I am empowered in all aspects of my life." When you decide what you want to say, write this someplace where you will see it every day, such as a bathroom mirror.

Though you can create this word of the year at any time of the year, it makes a good tradition for Samhain (considered the Pagan start of the new year) or New Year's Eve. This way you are setting your intention for the whole year. It can also be helpful to keep a list of past words. This is the kind of thing you could keep in your Book of Shadows or a magical journal, if you keep one.

HERBS FOR THE MIND

For centuries, and in countless cultures, the plants of the earth have been used to help heal a variety of ailments from fevers to skin conditions and even feelings such as fear and anxiety. For every sickness that exists in the world, nature has created a medicine. This is one of the ways balance is maintained in the world. It is up to each individual to decide how and when to integrate herbs into their own wellness practice. For some of you, herbal remedies used in conjunction with western medicine may be the path for you. For others, a completely herbal practice may be the way to go. And, for still others, herbal remedies will be skipped altogether. When making these decisions, please keep your safety in mind. Never ingest an herb if you don't know what it is. And, if you take medications, please ask your doctor about contraindications beforehand.

Many (not all) plants are generally regarded as safe. My personal experience with some of these herbs has been quite remarkable. It is worth noting that whenever you see the word *officinalis* in the botanical name of a plant, this plant was "officially recognized" for its health benefits as far back as the Roman empire.

- Anxiety: Passionflower (*Passiflora incarnate*), kava kava (*Piper methysticum*), lavender (*Lavandula angustifolia*), valerian (*Valeriana officinalis*), German chamomile (*Matricaria chamomilla*), Roman chamomile (*Chamaemelum nobile*), and lemon balm (*Melissa officinalis*).

- Depression: St. John's wort (*Hypericum perforatum*), valerian (*Valeriana officinalis*), passionflower (*Passiflora incarnata*), lavender (*Lavandula angustifolia*), saffron (*Crocus sativus*), hawthorn (*Crataegus monogyna*), lemon balm (*Melissa officinalis*), ginkgo biloba / maidenhair tree (*Ginkgo biloba*), and chamomile (*Matricaria chamomilla*).

- Stress: Ashwagandha (*Withania somnifera*), kava kava (*Piper methysticum*), lemon balm (*Melissa officinalis*), passionflower (*Passiflora incarnata*), lavender (*Lavandula angustifolia),* bacopa / water hyssop *(Bacopa monnieri),* chamomile (*Matricaria chamomilla*), valerian *(Valeriana officinalis*), and rhodiola (*Rhodiola rosea*).

- Mental clarity: Ginkgo biloba / maidenhair tree *(Ginkgo biloba),* rosemary (*Salvia rosmarinus*), lemon balm *(Melissa officinalis),* bacopa / water hyssop *(Bacopa monnieri),* gotu kola *(Centella asiatica),* sage *(Salvia officinalis),* ginseng *(Panax ginseng),* and green tea *(Camellia sinensis).*

- Brain health: Ginkgo biloba / maidenhair tree *(Ginkgo biloba),* rosemary (*Salvia rosmarinus*), holy basil (*Ocimum tenuiflorum*), ashwagandha (*Withania somnifera),* bacopa / water hyssop *(Bacopa monnieri),* lemon balm *(Melissa officinalis),* gotu kola *(Centella asiatica),* sage *(Salvia officinalis*), turmeric *(Curcuma longa),* and ginseng *(Panax ginseng).*

Many of the plants on this list can be bought in pill, tablet, liquid, or tincture form from any number of health food stores or online. In these variations, the recommended dosage should already be on the label. If you are more of the DIY type, dried and powdered versions of these herbs can be purchased at many metaphysical / occult / new age stores. These variations can be used as teas, incenses, and even cooked into meals. Though I must warn you, sometimes they taste rather horrid. You can also choose to grow these plants yourself or harvest them. If you harvest them from the wild, please make sure that you follow safe and ethical guidelines for wildcrafting.

MEDITATION

The benefits of meditation have been well-documented, even in the modern era. Studies show that meditation, in its variety of forms, helps with anxiety, patience, improving awareness, improving cognitive function, increasing mindfulness, reducing stress, lowering heart rate, and so much more. If you do not yet have a meditation practice, now is a great time to get one. The type of meditation you do should depend on you level of comfort, preference, and goals. Some of the practices discussed here are guided meditations, mindfulness meditations, movement meditations, and more. These will give you a basic idea of the types of meditation you can do.

Guided

There are literally thousands of guided meditations available on YouTube. Even better, there are many for specific needs, like mental clarity, stress reduction, better sleep, and grounding. When you are first starting off, wear comfortable clothes and start small. Maybe five minutes is all you can manage, so start there. If you are more experienced, find something at your level. If visualization is not your strong suit, guided meditations can provide a way to strengthen this skill.

Mindfulness

A mindfulness meditation is helpful to understand the patterns and symbols that occur frequently within your mind. If you are ever going to change thought patterns that are not supportive, you must first know they are there. Then you must learn to accept these thoughts without judgment. To do this, one of the most common ways is to focus on your breath. Don't try to force your breath, just let air flow in and out of your lungs. When a thought comes into your mind, acknowledge it then return to your breathing. After some time, you should notice common trends in your thinking. By being more aware of them when you meditate, you can become more aware of them in your waking state.

Movement Meditations

Have you ever done gardening, woodworking, or similar physical tasks and found that hours passed by in what seemed like mere minutes? This is because you were in a meditative state brought on through physical activity. One of the goals of meditation is to quiet the mind so we can receive answers from either our higher self or the Divine. Undertaking an action that allows us to go into a type of mental autopilot makes space for our subconscious minds to take over and strengthen this connection. This type of meditation can be done with a lot of different actions, but I find digging in the earth with my hands to be especially effective.

Body Scan

In a body scan meditation, you will check in with each part of your body, one-by-one, to look for discomfort, pain, or general lack of ease. Start at your feet and ask yourself how they feel. Then move up to your shins and calves and repeat the process. Work all the way up your body, section by section. When you reach an area of tension, pain, or discomfort, take a deep breath in, and, as you breathe out, see that area loosening, releasing, and healing. When you make it to the top of your head, take another deep breath in and release any tension that remains in your body. Take a few moments to become aware of your surroundings, and when you feel ready, open your eyes.

Clear Mind Meditation

In a clear mind meditation, try to keep thoughts from entering your mind. This meditation is recommended if you have a hard time focusing on one thought at a time. You will sit or lay down comfortably and close your eyes. When a thought comes into your mind, acknowledge it, then dismiss it. This meditation is more challenging than it sounds, so avoid getting angry if you can't do it or can't do it for very long. If you achieve a few seconds, that is awesome. This meditation is so helpful because if have no control over your thoughts, then you are being controlled by them and won't be able to focus enough to direct magic.

THINKING POWER

It is remarkable what the human brain is capable of. From reading to composing symphonies to coordinating the muscles necessary to tie our shoes, our brains can achieve almost anything. To keep our brains healthy and functioning at full capacity, we need to exercise them and get them out of their normal routine. We need to teach them to think in new ways. Fortunately, there are many ways to accomplish this.

Read Challenging Books

Does this mean that you need to pick up some work from Shakespeare or Beowulf on your way home? Or some large book on calculus? You can, but these aren't the only books that can be challenging. Let's say that you usually read romantic fiction; reading nonfiction or sci-fi could be challenging for you. If you have a smaller vocabulary than you want, try a book that is going to make you look up words to understand it. Challenging should be based on the question "What is challenging for me?" If you want some classically challenging books, you may want to consider books by Charles Dickens, Leo Tolstoy, Voltaire, Charlotte Brontë, Emily Brontë, or Nathaniel Hawthorne, among others.

Games and Puzzles

Games, such as chess, or jigsaw puzzles increase your cognitive function. Ideally, the games and puzzles you play shouldn't be too easy. They should take some thought. That doesn't mean they can't be fun though. Some games and puzzles that are known to be supportive of brain health include sudoku, chess, crossword puzzles, jigsaw puzzles, concentration or multitasking games. There are many apps that are designed to help improve cognition as well. Try a few out and you are sure to find one that you like.

Tai Chi

In a study done in 2013, it was found that tai chi could enhance sleep quality, reduce stress, and, drumroll please, improve memory. Tai chi has long been associated with mental health because of the structural changes it makes in the brain.[2] One of the best things about tai chi (aside from the fun factor) is that there are so many YouTube videos available. This means you can have a tai chi session anywhere that you have internet connection. Because it is a slow movement, low-impact workout, it is a good option for those with physical restrictions.

Classes and Lectures

You don't have to sign up for a bachelor's degree program right out of prison (although you can) to take advantage of higher

2. Sara Lindberg, "Brain Exercises: 13 Ways to Boost Memory, Focus, and Mental Skills," Healthline (Healthline Media, August 7, 2019), https://www.healthline.com/health/mental-health/brain-exercises.

learning. Depending on where you live, your local university may offer free or inexpensive introductory classes. Bookstores, libraries, and community buildings may host, or know about, local lectures. And, of course, do not forget to check online. Some of my favorite lectures have been from European universities and presented through video. They didn't cost me a thing except an hour of my time, and the payoff was worth it ten-fold.

Learn a New Skill

This is the time, today, right now, to hone your current skills and develop new ones. Don't worry about what anybody will think of you or any of the naysayers you may have encountered in the past. You *can* do this. Skills can be practical, such as public speaking, speed reading, learning a new language, or using a specific software. They can be magical, like spinning wool, candlemaking, or rune carving. They can be any kind of skill you want, really. Just don't be surprised if it turns into a hobby; that is a good thing!

EMOTIONAL HEALTH

Understanding your emotional health is just as important as understanding any other aspect of your mind and mental health. Sadly though, people tend to either ignore emotional health or have never been taught about emotional health in the first place. Just as there is a way to measure intelligence (IQ), there is a way to measure your emotional intelligence (EQ). Unlike an IQ test though, an EQ test doesn't have a set of numerical parameters. Instead, there are categories that are identified with EQ. The more able you are to utilize each of these categories, the higher your EQ. While EQ only makes up a piece of your emotional health, it is an important piece.

There are five main components to emotional intelligence: self-awareness, self-regulation, social skills, empathy, and motivation.[3] Here is where we will look at the meaning of each of these terms and how they apply to Paganism. But first, why should you care? Isn't this book about magic, mysticism, and communing with nature? You should care for a few reasons. First, if you've been to prison, there's a good chance you didn't learn these skills as effectively as you could have. Second, the faiths that fit under Paganism have an emphasis on personal accountability and growth. We don't get to simply pray for absolution on our death beds, our actions have consequences right now. Third, you deserve to have a healthy mind and emotions that don't rule over you and make decisions for you. Care about your emotional health because it enables you to make decisions based on rational thought instead of being based on anger or fear.

Self-Awareness

When talking about emotional self-awareness, it refers to the ability to identify what emotions you are feeling. It is unfortunate that so many people are raised to believe that the only acceptable emotions are angry and happy. There are so many nuances of emotion and so many words to express these emotions. When you are in a pleasant mood, you may feel happy, content, peaceful, jubilant, or lively. When emotions are unpleasant, you may be feeling fearful, somber, wistful, offended, or outraged. By expanding your knowledge of different emotions, you can more effectively communicate what you are feeling. Imagine being in a conversation with

---

3. "Emotional Intelligence in Leadership: Learning How to Be More Aware," MindTools, accessed September 5, 2021, https://www.mindtools.com/pages/article/newLDR_45.htm.

someone and being able to express to them, "Your actions make me feel betrayed," instead of "I'm angry." Though both are valid, the first one gives you a framework to open communication and to resolve the issue at its core. Self-awareness includes being able to acknowledge and admit your strengths and your weaknesses.

Magical Aspect

Identifying your emotions and knowing which ones you are trying to access helps you tap into them during magical workings. For example, if you are doing a love spell, you could focus on the feeling of love. If you are doing a job spell, you could focus on the sense of pride and relief you will have when you get hired. Emotions are quite powerful when they are harnessed correctly.

Putting It into Practice

Expand your emotional vocabulary to include more complicated emotions. Use these words instead of general and broad emotions (sad, happy) to describe how you are feeling.

Self-Regulation

Now that you have identified what emotions you are feeling, the next part of emotional intelligence is to not make decisions when you are in the grasp of intense emotions. Look, you are allowed to be angry or hurt or ecstatic or any other emotion you may be feeling. But anytime you are emotionally charged, whether the emotions feel good or don't, you are apt to make decisions that are not in your best long-term interest. If your boss tells you something you don't want to hear, it may cause you to feel embarrassed. This does not give you the right to flip them off or yell at them or throw a temper tantrum in the middle of work. What you can do is walk out to your car and scream, yell, and cuss until your heart is content. You can wait until you get home and journal about it. You can do a lot of things. Your emotions won't kill you. Let yourself be uncomfortable for a little bit.

Magical

It is almost cliché to hear about a person getting broken up with and wanting to do a love spell to get them back or being wronged in another way and wanting to hex that person. Stop it! These never work out the way you thought they would on the best of days. They are especially ineffective if you are teary, frustrated, angry, heartbroken, and hurting.

Putting It into Practice

Sit with your emotions. Being sad doesn't feel good; that's okay. You don't get to pick and choose which emotions you want to feel; it is an all or nothing deal. So, feel them. Talk to trusted friends or family or pets about those emotions. Just know it is okay to not be okay.

Social Skills

There is a certain level of tact that should be employed when dealing with other people. Now, while there are social cues and accepted norms in any given society, if you have been living in a cell or halfway house for a while, it might take some practice to get used to reading these signs again. How you interact with people in the "real world" can open or close doors for you. But don't let this scare you. All you must do is work on it a little bit at a time. One mistake I see people make is trying to be something they are not. Use your personality. If you are naturally introverted, then this might mean you take time before responding to others. Ergo, you may be a better listener than speaker. Who doesn't like a good listener? If you are uncomfortable in small groups, be part of larger ones or vice versa.

Magical Aspect

You can absolutely be a solitary practitioner, no problem. At some point though, you may want to attend a public Pagan gathering. Pagans tend to be a laid-back bunch. If you are nervous because you have never been to a public function before, that's okay. My experience has always been that after a few minutes of mingling in magical energy, I feel my body relax. If this doesn't happen, go find someone, be honest, and tell them, "This is my first gathering. I'm nervous." Most of the time they will be all too happy to help you feel welcome.

Putting It into Practice

To really practice being in social situations, one does have to be in social situations. However, you can practice things like listening and making conversation with almost anyone.

Empathy

Empathy simply means being able to understand another person's emotions. More people than ever before are acknowledging themselves as empaths. This really isn't surprising. We're supposed to be able to pick up on emotions of others. It is one of the things that allowed early human to form societies. Where it gets tricky is that many people are such strong path empaths that their own emotions get overshadowed by what they are picking up from others. Some of you reading this will completely understand how that feels.

But what if you don't have this skill or don't know how to access it? Chances are you do have this skill it just isn't that strong or you are not aware of it. You can practice empathy with a friend and some flash cards. Sit with your backs toward each other but not touching. In front of them will be a stack of flashcards with different emotions. One at a time, they will pick up a card and try to display that emotion on their face, body, and if they can get their energy to match that emotion, all the better. Then have them face you. Guess the emotion. This won't be a perfect representation, but if you struggle with empathy, it is a starting point.

Magical Aspect

If you are working with others, being able to read the emotions of your group can help you pick up on the emotional state of those working in ritual with you. The high priestess, high priest, or another designated person will usually be the one who makes sure that everybody's emotions and energies are flowing correctly. You can use empathy to "read" the emotional energy of a place before you enter it.

Putting It into Practice

Ground, center, and shield. Practice it a lot. This is discussed in the protection chapter. Once you get really good at it, you will find that your body will do it automatically or with minimal effort.

Motivation

Why are you doing the things you are doing? What motivates you? Are you learning about Paganism because you are bored? Do you feel called to the Pagan path? Are you curious? To clarify, none of these are "wrong" reasons. What motivates us to do things in life really relates to what we value in life. If you value education, then you may be learning about Paganism to fill a thirst to know more. If you value family, you may be learning about it so you can plan sabbats with your children. If you value connectedness, maybe that is what you seek with a Pagan circle. It doesn't really matter what your motivations are; the point is simply to understand them. It's okay if your motivations are focused on self. Altruism is great but taking care of yourself must be a priority. Doing something for you because it makes you feel good is fine, provided it doesn't take away from another's safety, security, or autonomy.

Magical Aspect

Really think about your motivation before you start planning rituals or spells. Your true motives will be known by the entities you call on to aid you, and it will impact your magic. Most of your rituals and spells will have honest motivations behind them. Getting a job: there's probably honest motives there. Protection, warding, grounding: these generally are motivated by security and safety. What I am talking about are the things like loves spells and spells based on vengeance disguised vaguely as justice. I'm talking about using your religion to cause others harm. Yes, I know some religions do just that, but be better than that. Be the magic you want to see in the world.

Putting It into Practice

Check in with yourself. Ask yourself the hard-hitting questions, why am I doing this spell? What outcome am I hoping for? Is the outcome I want harmful? Are there other ways to achieve my goal? Is this a goal I even *really* want to achieve?

EMOTIONAL STATE AND MAGIC

You may have heard not to do magic when you are angry or sad or emotionally charged in anyway. This relates to focus but also to your ability to decide if you should do the spell you intend.

The intent you put behind your magic has a big impact on the outcome. If you are angry for one reason or another, you will be sending out more anger into the world and be returned with anger. If you are doing a spell to be vindictive, this will have negative implications for you as well. Once the spell is cast, your emotional state is still important. If you find yourself in a frantic or obsessive state waiting for the spell to come into fruition, then you are letting air out of the balloon.

It should be stated that spell work should not be done when you are angry or upset or otherwise emotionally skewed. This alters your intent. For example, if you have just experienced something and you are in tears, you will not be able to focus your intention, may not even know what your intention is, nor will you be practicing proper self-care. You can, however, make yourself a tea or carry a stone to help ground yourself. You can still talk about your feelings and you can certainly take some deep breaths. Avoid doing any sort of magical work that is intent on retribution or assigning blame. I promise you these spells don't work out at the best of times, and they are an utterly disastrous when your emotions are out of tune.

DEALING WITH STRESS

Volumns of books have been written about stress and how it impacts our bodies and our mental health. In a nutshell, our brains chemically do not know the difference between the stress of running from a lion and the stress of having a deadline at work. The physiological response to each of these is the same. What this means is that digestion, sleep, cognitive function, emotional processing, coordination, reproductive functions, memory, and other areas are all impacted by stress. Yes, being stressed can negatively impact your mental health. Anything that is not necessary for immediate survival (running from a lion), will either function at a diminished capacity or not at all. In our modern world, most people live in an almost constant state of stress. Taking time to de-stress is one step that can help restore function and get your body and mind back to homeostasis.

Meditate

The details of this were discussed earlier in this chapter. I have provided a meditation to help you de-stress at the end of this chapter (page 51).

Aromatherapy

Scent is powerful. Does the smell of freshly baked cookies remind you of your grandma's house? Does the morning after a rainstorm fill you with feelings of elation? How about fresh-cut grass? What feelings and memories do various smells bring to mind? You can utilize scents to increase your mental capacity, calm yourself down, focus your attention, direct your magic and much more.

A scent has the ability to impact areas of your brain directly. For example, a scent can interact with your hypothalamus, which plays a major role in handling stress. Scents are also shown to improve depression symptoms and alleviating anxiety.[4] If you use essential oils for aromatherapy, they should only be used topically; that means don't eat or drink them. If you are using them in the bath, limit their use to just a few drops. When you inhale essential oils, do not hold the bottle up to your nose, instead hold it a few inches from your nose and waft the scent up using your hand. Some of the best ones to use to combat stress include lavender,

---

4. Nayana Ambardekar, "Aromatherapy & Essential Oils for Relaxation and Stress Relief," WebMD, last updated January 23, 2020, https://www.webmd.com /balance/stress-management/aromatherapy-overview#1.

neroli, ylang-ylang, bergamot, chamomile, sweet orange, and clary sage.

Practice Saying No

If you are so overwhelmed by obligations and commitments that you feel like you barely have time to breathe, then saying no can become a lifesaver. It is much less stressful to have a few things going on in your life that you can commit to completely than to have dozens of projects and never feel like you are accomplishing anything. This also makes it easier to handle random conflicts that can occur. If you are already stretched so thin that you can't breathe, small things can push you over the edge. This can lead to making decisions that are not thought all the way through. Decide what is important to you and make time for those things. Everything else you can decide on a case-by-case basis whether it is worth your energy and time.

Journal

Writing is such a therapeutic practice. There is something about putting pen to paper and letting all your thoughts flow that helps you gain a complete view of a situation. This practice works best if you do it regularly, at least three to five times per week. Periodically, go back through and read old journal entries. Did your viewpoint on a situation change? How did it get resolved?

Music

Music can let us feel, change our mood, or lift us up when we're down. Music is powerful and reminiscent of a time when humans sat around the fire 42,000 years ago with the first known instrument, hand-carved flutes.[5] Some of my times of greatest inspiration and relaxation come when I am listening to instrumental music. And it changes depending on my mood and intention.

> Note to PO:
>
> The parolees you work with on a day-to-day basis are under considerable stress. While we all have stress in our lives, try to remember that the formerly incarcerated population often has childhood trauma and has lived a life filled with stress. As those who were formally incarcerated transition to freedom, they are experiencing a new stress: the stress that comes from trying to change everything they have ever known. Consider the mental health of an individual, their efforts, and their needs.

A DE-STRESS MEDITATION

Get comfortable, either laying down or sitting comfortably. Take a few deep breaths in and out (at least three). Mentally, go over each part of your body one by one, starting with your feet, and ask yourself how each part feels. You probably know that an area that is tense is holding stress. But areas that are too cold, too hot, or just feel "off" can also hold stress. When you hit an area that is carrying stress, take a deep breath. This time, as you breathe in, breathe into that area. For example, you might breathe into your feet. As you breathe out, let the stress exit with your breath. Stay in one area until you feel like the stress is gone, then move on to the next. When you get to your head, remove the stress. Visualize a pentagram over your forehead. It will serve as a stress blocker.

---

5. BBC staff, "Earliest Music Instruments Found," *BBC News*, May 25, 2012, https://www.bbc.com/news/science-environment-18196349.

Then, take three big breaths in and out, and slowly become aware of your body and the room you are in. When you feel ready, open your eyes.

As this section on mental health closes out, I just want to provide a reminder that the health of your mind is very important and should not be neglected. If you need to enlist the aid of a professional, please do so. I do not encourage self-medicating, using illicit substances, or engaging in any sort of harmful behavior. What I do encourage is for you to reach out for support. With this in mind, you will find a list of resources for mental health in the back of this book (page 239). It is not a comprehensive list but can give you a good start.

CHAPTER 3
PHYSICAL HEALTH AND MAGIC

You have a sacred duty to take care of yourself. I'm sure many of you have spent a lot of time trying to take care of other people. You may have tried to pull someone out of the proverbial fire so many times that you find it hard to identify who you are without another person to serve as a pivot point. Now is the time to take care of your needs, to treat yourself as a sacred and valuable part of the cosmos. It is not selfish; it is necessary. You are no good to anyone if you are not getting your own needs met. Prison and jail doctors, while well meaning, do not always have the time or funding to provide the services you truly need. Part of the freedom you are now gaining comes with the price of maintenance. Maintenance in this context applies to keeping your mental, physical, and spiritual sides healthy and balanced. If you were recently incarcerated, then it is very likely that a checkup (at the minimum) is in order. I can hear some of you groaning and saying things like "I don't like doctors," "In my family, we don't go to doctors," and other similar such things. There are many social and cultural misconceptions about the doctor, wellness, health, and their connections. While I will not attempt to deconstruct myth and fact in this book, I will say that my years studying integrative healthcare have taught me that doctors have a time a place.

In addition to those we usually associate with doctors (allopathic medicine), there are also naturopathic doctors, homeopaths, herbalists, acupuncturists, and others who practice holistic healing modalities. Health and wellness encompass so much more than they used to. For me, the most amazing part is that our own roles in wellness are being recognized. Where patients used to be passive participants in healthcare, now patients have a voice and can now take part in preventative care and a growing field known as lifestyle medicine. Lifestyle medicine is what we'll talk about first.

LIFESTYLE MEDICINE

Lifestyle medicine has a big focus on preventative care. What if I told you that 80 percent of chronic diseases are completely preventable?[6] How would knowing that change your approach to health? If you knew that you could make changes in your life and prevent diseases like cancer, diabetes, heart disease, cardiovascular disease, or asthma, wouldn't you make the changes? Well, most people do know this. We have been taught since grade school that we should eat right, exercise regularly, get enough sleep, and that we shouldn't smoke. Sadly, most people still won't make these changes unless they are put into a situation where they no longer have a choice.

There are many theories as to why these changes won't occur. Dispelling some of the myths has shown to be a helpful tool to use when encouraging change. Ultimately though, you must be willing to make changes. Now, let's look at some of these areas and

---

6. Partnership to Fight Chronic Disease, "The Growing Crisis of Chronic Disease in the United States," fightchronicdisease.org (Partnership to Fight Chronic Disease), accessed 2020, https://www.fightchronicdisease.org/sites/default/files/docs/GrowingCrisisofChronicDiseaseintheUSfactsheet_81009.pdf.

improvements you can make that are manageable. Think of these as starting points.

Diet

Your body is a temple. To honor the gods, treat it as such. In the context of this book, diet will refer to nutrition and eating patterns, not the practice of weight loss, as the word is frequently tied to. You are likely to hear so many opinions on what diets are the best for you, and that can feel overwhelming. The good news is that you do not have to become a super vegan, eat all organic, or grow your food to improve your diet. Just do one thing to start but do it consistently.

Reducing Soda

Soda is full of sugar, caffeine, additives, and a whole bunch of other stuff your body doesn't like. If you are not ready to cut it out completely, reduce how much you drink per day for six months, then reduce it again and again. Diet soda is just as bad for you (some studies suggest it's worse) than regular soda. Don't be fooled; diet soda does nothing to help with weight loss.

Reduce Energy Drinks

Energy drinks are a misnomer. While they give you a short burst of energy, they make you more tired in the long run. Use the reduction method listed under soda to wean yourself off.

Eat More Vegetables

If you are one of those people who "just doesn't like vegetables," you have probably never had them properly prepared. Yeah, a raw piece of broccoli slapped willy-nilly on your plate is not that appealing. But a well-seasoned vegetarian fajita, now that is scrumptious. When you are adding vegetables, try to get as many different colors on your plate as possible. Foods that come directly from the earth have a stronger connection to earth energy than those that are processed, canned, or altered.

Eat More Fruit

We all get cravings for sweet foods sometimes. Next time one hits, grab a piece of fruit instead of a candy bar. If you want to have pre-prepared snacks, oven bake some sliced strawberry slices or invest in a food dehydrator. Dried fruit can be every bit as sweet as candy, and when you make it yourself, you know all the ingredients that went into it. Magically, fruits are connected to the elements of water and earth.

Hara Hachi Bu

This is a Japanese term that translates roughly to "eat until you are 80 percent full." To do this, you will need to eat slowly and not rush your meal. This has a few benefits on its own including slowing down, mindfulness, portion control, and savoring the flavors of your food. In Okinawa, where this term originates, the population has low rates of heart disease, stroke, and cancer as well as a long life expectancy compared to other areas.[7]

Exercise

Here is another one of those words that people either embrace or turn their head to pretend they didn't hear it. Exercise does not have to be scary, expensive, or rigid. Some of you developed work-

7. Ann Milanowski, "Don't Eat Until You're Full—Instead, Mind Your Hara Hachi Bu Point," Health Essentials from Cleveland Clinic (Health Essentials from Cleveland Clinic, September 4, 2020), https://health.clevelandclinic.org/dont-eat-until-youre-full-instead-mind-your-hara-hachi-bu-point/.

out routines while you were locked up; don't lose them! Those of you who did not, that's okay. Like most things in life, it is progress, not perfection, that matters. Do not fear, it doesn't have to be painful. It can be quite pleasant. You just need to find a routine that works for you and your goals.

Walk

Walking is free. Some cities have beautiful walking trails or parks. You can walk to the store instead of driving or walk around your local gym. When you walk, do it at a brisk pace instead of a leisurely stroll so that your heart gets pumping. You can apply this same principle to jogging, running, bike riding, roller blading, and more.

Tai Chi, Yoga, and Martial Arts

While each of these is different, they all give your body a workout while also having benefits for your mind. If the idea of running for miles does not appeal to you, tai chi, yoga, or martial arts might. These practices increase focus, flexibility, and put you in tune with your breath, which is important for any spiritual or magical practice. There are great starter videos online.

Dance

For me, dance is primal. There are times, most times, when I hear a beat and feel it making its way through my bones and into my core, and I have no choice but to move my body to the music. Please don't fall into the trap of thinking you need to be a professional dancer to dance. This may be true for ballroom-style competitions, but almost anybody can move. Even if you are putting on music in your home and dancing around your living room, this is getting your blood pumping and your spirit moving. So, dance!

Get a Workout Buddy

In whatever way you decide to get your exercise, consider having a workout buddy. If you are supposed to meet your friend at a certain time each week, then you are more likely to keep up with your workout routine or commitment. It also adds an element of fun for both of you. You might even find a hiking group or something. Talk about a great way to build community!

Sleep

It is not just the amount of sleep you get in hours but the quality of your sleep that allows your body to heal, mend, and reset. The average adult needs seven to nine hours of sleep each night to function properly. I hear a lot of people say that they feel rested on just a few hours of sleep, but research shows that people who get less than the recommended amount of sleep do not perform as well on complex tasks compared to those who do.[8] I have listed some magical suggestions for helping you sleep. Feel free to look up some more mundane ones and incorporate those as well.

Meditate before Bed

Whether it is guided meditation, breath work, or something else entirely, any kind of meditation is wonderfully calming. If you fall asleep, it means that your body needed the sleep. Don't fret about it; you got exactly what was intended.

---

8. Eric J. Olson, "How Many Hours of Sleep Do You Need?" Mayo Clinic (Mayo Foundation for Medical Education and Research, June 6, 2019), https://www .mayoclinic.org/healthy-lifestyle/adult-health/expert-answers/how-many -hours-of-sleep-are-enough/faq-20057898.

Tea

There are some wonderful teas available on the market that are designed to help with sleep. Usually they contain lavender, chamomile, or valerian root. You can also brew your own combining these and other ingredients. Do not mindlessly drink it down; instead, sip it slowly, and become aware of the herbs relaxing your body and mind, preparing yourself for sleep.

Deep Breathing

There is almost nothing that cannot be made better by deep and intentional breathing. It reduces feelings of fear and anxiety, and can be useful in helping you manage moods, thoughts, and increasing your awareness of the present. Breathe intentionally and deeply whenever possible, but especially when you need to sleep after a long day.

Pillow Sachet

I keep a small bag with an amethyst stone in it in my pillow. Periodically, I add a few drops of lavender oil to the bag. These help me to sleep peacefully and dream well. I also keep a selenite wand in my bed frame to aid in the redistribution of my energies while I sleep. You can add anything you would like to your pillow sachet.

Water

However much water you drink, it is likely not enough. We come from the waters of the womb, reminiscent of the seas in which life first arose. An interesting factoid I learned in my anatomy and physiology class years ago is that anything that is not water processes in the body as food. If you are drinking coffee, tea, juice, soda, any of it, you are eating as far as your body is concerned. Think about what this means for weight management, let alone the other physiological bodily processes. This is one of those areas where you can set a small goal, then another, and another. If drinking water isn't something you normally do, aim for one or two glasses a day for a few weeks, then increase it.

HOLISTIC MODALITIES

Allopathic medicine is what most people think of when they think of a doctor. Treatments for disease that are not allopathic are called holistic, also known as alternative medicine, alternative modalities, natural medicine, or folk medicine. Though some people in the scientific and medical communities are still skeptical about the efficacy of alternative healing, I encourage you to decide for yourself. I have had some amazing personal experiences with Traditional Chinese Medicine, herbal remedies, and energy medicine. Over the years, these have become my go-tos for general maintenance. I still go to allopathic doctors when needed, but these alternative methods have saved me many trips.

There is a misconception that if you are using alternative healing methods, you are going to a person who is not trained. This is simply not true. Each of the modalities mentioned below has their own method of training and credentialing body. Some require a certificate where others will have a more formal education. You always have a right to ask the practitioner about their credentials and to ask questions about those credentials. Any credible practitioner should be more than willing to provide this information. Most will even list it on their website.

Traditional Chinese Medicine

Traditional Chinese Medicine has been used in China for over two thousand years. Some of the techniques used include acupuncture, dietary changes, herbal supplements, cupping, moxibustion, and movement practices such as tai chi, to balance the elements, restore qi flow, and balance out yin and yang energy. Any legitimate practitioner should have their credentials available upon request, if not displayed already. It takes up to four years of postgraduate study to be licensed in Traditional Chinese Medicine.

Homeopathy

Though people will frequently use homeopathic and holistic as synonyms, they are not the same. Homeopathy is a specific and distinct modality that has two basic premises. The first is that "like cures like." This means that something that causes a specific symptom in a healthy person can also treat it in a sick one. The second is the "law of minimum dose." [9] Some homeopathic remedies are distilled and filtered time and time again so that the essence of the original substance remains, but they are so heavily diluted that the substance no longer causes harm. At many health-food stores you can find homeopathic creams, salves, ointments, tablets, and more. While homeopathic practitioners don't necessarily have to have certification, there are certification programs that many elect to take.

Naturopathic Doctor

A naturopath, or naturopathic doctor, is a fully licensed doctor. In fact, the first couple of years they spend in medical school are the same an allopathic doctor would take. It is the last couple of years that focus more on massage, exercise, nutrition, homeopathy, herbal medicine, and other holistic treatments, making this where the difference lies. Instead of treating a disease or a set of

---

9. "Homeopathy," National Center for Complementary and Integrative Health, last updated July 2018, https://www.nccih.nih.gov/health/homeopathy.

symptoms, a naturopathic doctor will focus on the wellness of their patient's body, mind, and spirit. They are likely to work in collaboration with other specialists to provide more well-rounded care. The downside of a natruopathic doctor is that they are not able to practice in every state, only those that recognize their licensure. If you are in a state that has natruopathic doctors, it is not a guarantee that insurance will cover your visit.

Doctor of Osteopathic Medicine

Just like a naturopathic doctor, an osteopathic doctor focuses on treating the whole body, not just specific ailments. An osteopathic doctor will focus on the musculoskeletal system and the impact it has on the rest of the body. For examples, frequent migraines may be occuring due to a misalignment of the spine down by the pelvis. Therefore, by using massage, stretching exercises, and medication when needed, the cause of the issue can be addressed. Doctors of osteopathic medicine are licensed in all fifty states and go through extensive medical training.

Energy Medicine

Energy is one of the topics I find most fascinating. Our bodies are energy. The stars, the planets, and our thoughts are all energy. Our cells, which seem so still and solid, are really in a state of constant vibration because they, too, are energy. Even "solid" objects vibrate on a molecular level. Have you ever picked up an object and immediately gotten a "feeling" from it? Well, this is because you felt how that object was vibrating; you literally felt its energy.

When this idea is applied to physical health, you must consider that all those streetlights, cell phones, other people, songs on the radio, chemicals in the air, the food we eat, *everything* is also vibrating and interacting with our bodies. Depending on our sensitivities and what self-care we use, our bodies can change their energy field (gain or lose electrons) and carry a charge just from the daily interaction we have.[10] When this exposure is prolonged, it can lead to physical problems which can range from anxiety to cancer. Before you start panicking though, there are ways to restore your body's energy level to where it is supposed to be, and they are surprisingly easy. Here are just a few of the more common ones.

Earthing

Think about the last time you went outside and stood on some grass barefoot with the sun shining down on your face. How did you feel? You probably felt pretty good. Earthing is as simple as being outside and walking barefoot on the earth or putting your hands palms down on the ground and letting them connect to the earth for a few moments. Use naturaly-occurring ground whenever possible: grass, dirt, and leaves as opposed to concrete or vinyl flooring.

Chakras

Chakras are energy centers of the body. Chakras are a concept originally found in Hinduism and other spiritual views from India. Though we most commonly hear about seven chakras, other traditions will use as few as five or as many as twenty-eight chakra centers. The seven chakras each correspond to a color and a physical part of the body. For example, the heart chakra (anahata), which is in the center of your chest just to the right of your heart, has a color of green or pink. When this chakra is blocked, your

---

10. James L. Oschman, "Chapter 17. Energy Medicine in Daily Life," in *Energy Medicine: The Scientific Basis*, 2nd ed. (Edinburgh: Elsevier, 2016), 297–330.

heart, lungs, and arms can be affected. It can also restrict your ability to experience self-love.

Aura

The energy of our bodies is not just within our cells. It extends outward in all directions. The aura is like having an orb of energy that surrounds us. In fact, it is exactly like that. It is not just humans but all biological matter that have auras. In the example above, where you pick up an object and get immediate impressions, it is the aura of that item that you are working with. With practice, you can learn to see auras and what color they are. But if you know how to listen for it, almost everyone can detect an aura with practice.

Reiki

Reiki, as it is practiced now, is a fairly recent form of energy work in terms of development. Its creation is attributed to Dr. Mikao Usui in 1922, but it is worth noting that during this time there were other versions of Reiki being practiced in Japan.[11] Reiki is a method of opening the energy channel so that one can be a vessel for healing energies. When performing Reiki, it is not your own energy that you use. It is the limitless energy of the universe that you are channeling through you. It is also worth noting that using energy to heal is a practice that is so old it is almost impossible to date. Reiki healers get attunements to signify what level they are: I, II, or III.

---

11. William Lee Rand, *Reiki: The Healing Touch, First and Second Degree Manual* (New Delhi India: Health Harmony, 2014), https://www.reiki.org/faqs /what-history-reiki.

Prayer

Don't let the association of prayer with other religions dissuade you from using it. Prayer is used to speak to the Divine, spirits, or ancestors. There is no monopoly on prayer. When a Witch casts a spell, this is a prayer. And prayers are thoughts, which are also energy. It is a bad habit to only pray when you need or want something. When I talk to the gods, I am frequently thanking them or checking in to see if they have any messages for me. Sometimes I pray for wisdom or strength or understanding. Most frequently, I am asking how I may be of service to them. There is no rule that says you cannot pray for physical things. But you might be surprised how much more filling the intangible requests become.

Laying On of Hands

The belief in the healing properties of touch have been well-documented in society since ancient Egypt.[12] Its use is also recorded in India, China, and Medieval Europe, where it was believed to cure scrofula, better known today as tuberculosis.[13] If you need more evidence of the healing power of touch, think about how it feels to get a hug from someone you love and trust when you are facing a hardship or when you have not seen that person in a long time. Human beings are creatures that thrive on connection. The brain chemistry and epigenetic changes that occur with touch are beyond the scope of this book. But this subject makes for fascinating reading if you want to give yourself something to do on a rainy afternoon.

12. Bob Reynolds, "In Every Land and Time: An Informal History of Hands-on Healing," LifeSpark Cancer Resources, August 28, 2018, https://www .lifesparknow.org/every-land-time-informal-history-hands-healing/.

13. Cengage, "Encyclopedia of Occultism and Parapsychology. Encyclopedia. com. 3 Mar. 2021.," Encyclopedia, accessed March 3, 2021, https://www .encyclopedia.com/science/encyclopedias-almanacs-transcripts-and-maps /healing-touch.

STONES FOR PHYSICAL WELL-BEING

Just as we see in the other chapters on health, stones have a place of prominence. When you carry a stone, you are welcoming its properties, healing and otherwise, to accompany you. But there are other ways to engage with the stone energy. There are glass water bottles available that have a clear base full of stones. You can screw on different bases to get different stone property effects. In this way you are taking in the energy of the stone internally. You can also promote healing while you sleep by making small stone pouches to put in your pillowcase.

Healing Stone Examples

Healing stones are worn, carried, kept in satchels, put in pillows, or otherwise kept close to one's body so that the vibration of the stone can resonate with your own energies. This helps the vibration of your body to align with the vibration of the stone to promote healing.

Obsidian

I love obsidian. Its glass-like appearance allows it to reflect the true nature of your ailment into the consciousness of your mind, meaning if you are not sure what exactly is wrong with your body, meditating with a piece of obsidian can help provide clarity. The smooth surface of obsidian can encourage the smooth flow of blood through your veins. It also helps with digestion and detoxifies. On a side note, obsidian is made when volcanic lava meets water and is quickly cooled. If you get a piece of obsidian with an air bubble, you have a representation of all four elements. This can help bring the elements within yourself into balance. See, there are many reasons to love obsidian.

Bloodstone

As the name indicates, this stone may be good for promoting blood flow, i.e., lowering blood pressure. It also wards off negative energies in the world around you and the world within you. Bloodstone is a great detoxifier. Many of us don't get to live away from the city and eat all-organic produce we grow ourselves. This means that we are exposed to oxidative chemicals in our day-to-day activities. Carrying a bloodstone or wearing jewelry made of bloodstone may help reduce the impact of these oxidative chemicals.

Unakite

Unakite has a variety of properties that could really place it within any of the healing chapters of this book. The reason it is included in physical health is because of its association with reproductive health and safe pregnancy. It may also help a person return to their normal physical state after a period of illness. Its other aspects include opening the third eye, grounding, and bringing spirit and emotions together. The latter is useful if you tend to let emotions rule your decisions.

Green Tourmaline

This is great stone for tapping into the sacred masculine and imbuing yourself with confidence and physical strength. It brings out the very best of masculine energy for the one who wears it. It is also associated with the heart and can help you to lower your heart rate and restore the nervous system to homeostasis. Because of its association with the heart, it is a good stone to carry with you after healing from heart surgery or in conjunction with hypertension and cardiovascular disease treatments.

Don't Forget Your Minerals

Perhaps the most important stones of all for physical health are the minerals that our bodies need to carry out daily functions. There are over one hundred minerals that our bodies need. If you have a diet that predominantly consists of plants, then many of these will make their way in through the food you eat. If your diet is heavy in sugar and processed food, then it is almost a guarantee that you are not getting enough minerals. The bacteria that live within our digestive tract have an impact on our emotions and the development of certain diseases and depend on nutrient-rich foods.[14] Make sure to get enough iron, selenium, magnesium, and zinc to keep everything functioning properly. Skin is our first line of defense against pathogens. To keep skin nourished, you want adequate amounts of copper, selenium, and zinc. For your bones, get plenty of calcium, iron, magnesium, and manganese.

HERBS FOR BODY HEALTH

It should go without saying, but I'll say it anyway: herbs are great but do not use "I take herbs," as a reason to avoid medical checkups and treatment. I'm a firm believer that both holistic and allopathic modalities have a time and a place. Herbs are great but so is getting an annual physical. When correctly applied, medicine of the past and medicine of the present can work together.

If you are on medication, pregnant, breastfeeding, have a serious medical condition, or are about to undergo surgery, please check with your doctor before downing gallons of herbal infusions. Also, be sure to do your research before taking any plant.

---

14. Adam Hadhazy, "Think Twice: How the Gut's 'Second Brain' Influences Mood and Well-Being," *Scientific American*, February 12, 2010, https://www.scientificamerican.com/article/gut-second-brain/.

Mistletoe twigs have healing properties, but the berries are quite poisonous. Horse chestnut and buckeye are virtually identical, the difference is one is toxic the other safe. Don't get me wrong, I love herbs. I use them for a lot of different things. During cold season, elderberry is my best friend. For pain, I am all about turmeric. Over the years, I have developed my go-tos for all sorts of physical ailments. The herbs listed here are ones that are likely to be safe and are sold commercially. Not all herbs should be taken internally. Aromatherapy is just as effective in many cases as teas. There are others, but that is research you will have to do on your own.

> *Heart health*: Green tea *(Camellia sinensis)*, hawthorn *(Crataegus* spp.*)*, olive leaf *(Olea europaea)*, garlic *(Allium sativum)*, reishi mushrooms *(Gandoerme lucidum)*, dandelion leaf *(Taraxacum officinale)*, cayenne *(Capsicum annuum)*, and rose (*Rosa* spp.*)*.

> *Inflammation/pain*: Cat's claw *(Uncaria tomentosa)*, thunder god vine *(Tripterygium wilfordii)*, chili peppers *(Capsicum annum)*, turmeric *(Curcuma longa)*, ginger *(Zingiber officinale)*, willow bark *(Salix* spp.*)*, black pepper *(Piper nigrum)*, Japanese knot weed *(Polygonum cuspidatum)*, and rosemary *(Salvia rosmarinus)*.

> *Brain health*: Ginkgo biloba/maidenhair tree *(Ginkgo biloba)*, rosemary *(Salvia rosmarinus)*, holy basil *(Ocimum tenuiflorum)*, ashwagandha *(Withania somnifera)*, bacopa/water hyssop *(Bacopa monnieri)*, lemon balm *(Melissa officinalis)*, gotu kola *(Centella asiatica)*, sage *(Salvia officinalis)*, turmeric *(Curcuma longa)*, and ginseng *(Panax ginseng)*.

Immune system (pre-infection): Elderberry *(Sambucus nigra)*, astragalus *(Astragalus propinquus)*, rhodiola *(Rhodiola rosea)*, goldenseal *(Hydrastis canadensis)*, maitake mushroom *(Grifola frondosa)*, angelica root *(Angelica archangelica)*, chamomile *(Matricaria chamomilla)*, ginger *(Zingiber officinale)*, andrographis *(Andrographis paniculata)*, and echinacea *(Echinacea angustifolia* and *purpurea)*.

Digestion: Peppermint *(Mentha × piperita)*, ginger *(Zingiber officinale)*, fennel *(Foeniculum vulgare)*, marsh mallow *(Althaea officinalis)*, plantain *(Plantago major)*, meadowsweet *(Filipendula ulmaria)*, sweet flag *(Acorus calamus)*, dandelion *(Taraxacum officinale)*, caraway *(Carum carvi)*, and calendula *(Calendula officinalis)*.

PHYSICAL POWER

Think of your body and all the flexibility, healing, moving, growing, changing, and rejuvenating it does in a lifetime. When was the last time you really let yourself be in your body, feel it, and enjoy it? I can hear some of you and I want to acknowledge that yes, pain and discomfort sometimes come with having a physical body on a physical plane. But I am still going to encourage you to try to be in your body, completely present. How? I am so glad you asked. The next few pages will list just some of the ways to be present. Before you begin, set your intention: "I am going to _____ in order to connect with my body," then proceed to do one of the following.

Stretch

Stretching is good for the lymphatic system. The lymphatic system often does not get the credit it deserves, it helps maintain fluid levels throughout your body. This sounds simple, but in the process, it fights off infections, removes toxins, and filters out bodily debris. When you stretch, it is like wringing out a wet towel, which gives the lymph system a boost.

Shower/Bathe with Intention

There are times when standing in the shower and staring off into space serve as a meditation. When was the last time you really let yourself experience the water falling onto your body or surrounding it? Water is cleansing and reminiscent of the safety of the womb in which we all begin life. Water is also healing, and if we are spiritually and mentally well, we tend to be more physically well.

Move Your Body

The health benefits of exercise are well documented. There are also many types ranging from running a 5K to yoga to tai chi to kickboxing. Even walking for fifteen minutes a few times per week will give your heart and your lungs a workout. The great thing about tai chi and other exercises is that there are videos you can find online. You don't need equipment for most of them. If you are a gym person, then lift, squat, pump, and move with intention.

Body Check-In

During a body check-in, ask each body part how it feels. I do this out loud but you can do it in your mind, if you prefer. Usually, it will go something like this: "Feet, how are you doing today?" I sit for a moment to hear the answer. Then I'll move up my body: "Shins, how are you doing today?" Again, I wait for the answer. I work all the way up my body and down my arms. When you reach a spot that is sore or uncomfortable, ask that area what it needs to feel better. Massage? Rest? Heat? Then give it that.

Mirror Affirmation

This next exercise should be done alone. It is about learning to love your body as it is. We all have those imperfections, those things that we initially don't like about ourselves. But these things that we tend to focus on with hypervigilance are what make us unique, one of a kind. Pick an area you normally critique. Maybe you have wished 1000 times to not have ears that are big. Look at this area of your body and say "I love you (ears). I accept that you are part of me and embrace your shape and form." Then, list three things out loud that you like or that are beneficial about this part of your body. With the ears example, you might list "I like the way you keep the hair out of my face."

SPELL FOR BODY AWARENESS

All the things listed under the physical power section can absolutely be magical acts. But I know that when I first learned about magic, I often felt like I was bursting out of my own skin. It took time for me to really step into my physical power. I invite you to try this spell. It can be illuminating to either accept your form as it is or to become aware of changes that would make you more comfortable.

What You Need

- Four taper candles, one for each cardinal direction: green or brown for north, yellow for east, red for south, and blue for west. You could also use four white candles instead.

- One of the following: a small hand drum, cymbals, or metronome. If these are not available, you may clap.
- A rubber band.
- Recently collected flower petals or silk cloth.
- A feather.
- Incense of your choosing.
- Incense holder.
- Matches or lighter.
- A candle snuffer. Alternatively, you can wet your fingers and pinch out the candles. Be careful not to burn yourself.

Start by setting one candle in the north, one in the east, one in the south, and one in the west.

For this spell you will face north, so place your items so they will be reachable when you sit down.

Starting in the north, go around the circle in a deasil (clockwise) direction with the lit incense while saying "I make this space safe for my body, a sanctuary for my mind, and temple for spirit." Set the incense in a holder.

Once again starting in the north and moving deasil, light each candle, one by one. As you light the north candle say, "My skin and my bones, energy of earth, you shape this home."

In the east say, "My thoughts and my mind, energy of air, you create things so sublime."

In the south say, "My blood and my passion, in me you live. Energy of fire, life's spark you give."

In the west say, "My emotions, hopes, and dreams, energy of water, be revealed to me."

Return to the north. Take a moment to be aware that all the elements are housed within your body. Then, sit comfortably on the floor, facing north.

Take a few deep breaths. Gently touch the flower petals or silk cloth, pick one up, rub it between your fingers. This represents your skin, soft, supple, and yet protective and strong. What are all the things that could describe how this flower petal feels? Gently rub it against your skin until you know that the petal and your skin are one in the same. When you feel this is complete, place the petals down and off to the side.

Next, pick up the rubber band. Stretch it and relax it. Put your fingers together and put the rubber band around the outside of your fingers. Expand and relax your fingers, feel the tension and relaxation. This represents your muscles moving, expanding, contracting, stretching. They make movement possible. As you stretch and relax the rubber band, stretch and relax certain muscles. How does it feel? Don't stretch too much now, you'll damage your muscles, your rubber band. We don't want it to snap. When you feel connected to all your muscles, set the rubber band aside.

Grab the hand drum or whatever item you'll be using and start tapping, softly and slowly at first. Try to listen or feel for your heartbeat, then match the drum to the beating of your own heart. This is the heartbeat of your ancestors, the beat of all those who have lived before and who will live after. They carry your blood, and you carry theirs. Ba-dumf dumf … ba-dumf dumf. Your heart is pumping blood through your body; feel it. Focus on it. Become one with it. Then, thank it for returning to your heart so the process can begin anew. Set your drum down knowing that your heart will continue to beat and pump and push the blood through your body.

Now, pick up the feather. It is your breath. Hold it between your fingers close enough to your face that you can see the feather move as you inhale and exhale (but not so close to make you sneeze). Breathe in and out as you watch the feather move. This is the power of breath, the power of words, the power of voice. You can make the physical world move with these things, so use them wisely. Change how deep and how fast you breath. What happens to the feather? Does it move less? Does it move more? Notice that you do not have to be loud to make the feather move. What does this mean for communication in your world? Spend time with the feather and your breath. When you are done, set the feather down.

Sit in front of the candle for a moment and fully return to your body. Become aware of your muscles and your skin and the floor. When you are ready, stand up and face north. This time, you will move widdershins (counterclockwise) from north to north. One by one, put the candles out with your snuffer or fingers. At each candle say:

> I am my heartbeat; I am my breath.
> I am my muscles, my skin, my health.
> My thanks to the elements for keeping my body running well.

At the end, I like to say "Huzzah," as a sign that the ritual is done and I am back in the mundane world.

CHAPTER 4
SPIRITUAL HEALTH AND MAGIC

We are spiritual beings having a physical experience. We are spirit. Sit and meditate on what that means for a moment. We *are* spirit. All the physical things, even our physical bodies, are finite. But our spirit is energy and therefore cannot be created nor destroyed. Only transformed. This chapter is about health and transformation of spirit. Human beings spent the bulk of our existence as a species living a life that was closely connected to the earth and the rhythms of nature. Most of modern societies are not connected to nature, spirit, the gods, and our cultural or blood ancestors like we once were. This has led to a spiritual sickness that, sadly, is very prevalent in our world. This spiritual disconnection leads to diseases of the body and mind.

Being spiritual means a lot of different things to different people. Some use it as a catch-all word. Others use it because they are uncomfortable with the word *religion* or feel that religion is a misrepresentation. For me, being spiritual means that I have never taken a step alone. Going to prison, though horrible, put me on a trajectory to live the life I live now. The lessons I needed to learn were there. In a weird way, it was a great gift. While you read this chapter on spiritual health, try not to have a limited and narrow view of what being spiritual can mean. Remember, even the most steadfast atheist can still feed their spirit. This chapter is about how to do just that.

WHAT DOES SPIRITUAL DIS-EASE LOOK LIKE?

There are many symptoms of spiritual dis-ease, meaning the body is out of a state of ease with itself. Once you are aware of it, you will see indicators in a lot of places. It comes in the form of flying off the handle over nothing. It comes in the form of manipulating a situation just because you can. It presents as not respecting another's boundaries, not being able to accept no for an answer, being constantly negative, and acting like no one else matters. There are many physical manifestations of spiritual sickness: drug use, self-harm, depression, isolation, overeating, anorexia/bulimia, codependence, and many, many others. Spiritual disease has an impact on our physical bodies and can cause acute and chronic health conditions of the body and mind if we don't heal it.

Now, don't get me wrong. We all get angry at times. It is perfectly natural. But how you handle that anger speaks a great deal to your spiritual state. There is a misnomer in society that being spiritual means that you must be "love and light" all the time. This is really ignoring a vital piece of yourself. No, I am not saying that you should resort to hexes as the first thing in your magical arsenal, but I am saying that it is okay to not be perfect. It is amazing to not be perfect. Being imperfect gives us the ability to grow and change and become a different person from where we were at a year ago or ten years ago. This ability to push ourselves to be a bit better than yesterday is one of the most amazing gifts that we are given. Honor that gift.

Years ago when I got out of prison, I was so angry all of the time. I was angry at people I knew and people I didn't. I was angry at the world and myself and organized religion and everything. It hurt to simply exist. I was in a state of spiritual dis-ease. What triggers this state will vary from person to person, but there are some common causes that tend to be at the root. If any of these apply to you, I promise you are not the only one. Not everyone who experiences the factors that follow will even find themselves in a state of spiritual disease but the percentage that will is quite high. The good news is that it is not your fault, and you are not to blame. You are not necessarily responsible for the factors that lead to spiritual dis-ease, but you are responsible for taking the steps to heal it. Let's look at some of these factors and put them into the context of spiritual health.

Trauma

Trauma is real. Don't let anyone tell you differently. Not only is it real but there is scientific documentation as to the effects it has on us. Trauma can be physical such as assault, rape, abuse, and similar things. But it can also happen in less tangible and harder-to-define ways. Examples of this could be being born into a family that didn't want you, having a family that wanted you to be a different sex, a family that does not support you if you come out, not living up to parental expectations, being bullied, being teased, being harassed—you get the idea.

Trauma physically changes our brains—especially when it happens in childhood—and can impact decision-making, emotional regulation, impulsivity, our ability to connect to others, our stress response, and more. According to the Centers for Disease Control, 60 percent of adults have experienced at least one traumatic event in their childhood and almost 25 percent have experienced three or more.[15] When you consider these numbers, it is not surprising that so many people live in a state of spiritual dis-ease.

Soul Loss

Simply put, soul loss is a disconnection from or damage to our spirit, our life essence. It can be brought on by trauma and frequently is. Soul loss can also occur because of choices we make. Depression is one of the most common symptoms. But you might also see chronic conditions occur, especially those that don't seem to have physical cause.

This is a difficult idea for Western culture to wrap its head around. It tends to think of diseases as having a biological or microbial origin more than a spiritual one. But throughout most of human history, the opposite is true. There are still shamanistic cultures in the world that acknowledge soul loss (or some variation) as causing addiction, inability to love or be loved, feeling fragmented, suicidal thoughts, general malaise, and more.[16]

Fear

With fear, it is important to make the distinction between the sense of fear a person gets when they are in a potentially dangerous situation and the chronic fear that prevents a person from moving forward and progressing in life. The fear we are talking about here is the latter. For some, it will be a fear of failure, for others, a fear of success. It may also be a fear of pain, fear of loss, fear of the unknown. These things can hold us in place. We can

15. CDC staff, "CDC Washington Testimony July 11, 2019," Centers for Disease Control and Prevention, last updated July 12, 2019, https://www.cdc.gov/washington/testimony/2019/t20190711.htm.

16. Hank Wesselman, "3 Causes of Spiritual Illness," Omega, last updated 2021, https://www.eomega.org/article/3-causes-of-spiritual-illness.

become comfortable in the uncomfortable and fight to stay there, not realizing that if we just let go, the doors would swing open.

We have all heard the expression "You can't teach an old dog new tricks"; well, it's rubbish! First, you are not a dog. Second, it is *never* too late to change. Sometimes you must be fearless. That doesn't mean not scared; it means not being inhibited by your fear. Life is a great adventure. I did not live completely on my own until I was thirty-four. I didn't even think that I could. Boyfriends, parents, couch-hopping, there had always been a safety net. When I did finally live on my own, I found out that not only could I live on my own, but I thrive on my own. Never for a moment let yourself think that I wasn't terrified at the time. I just asked the gods to protect me and took that first step.

Lack of Support

I want to tell you right now, in case no one else ever has, you *are* enough. You are. There are many of you who grew up without support. This could have been in the form of someone telling you to give up on your dreams, ignoring you, shunning you when you came out, or many other ways. When we are faced with a lack of support, it impacts our internal dialogue—the way we speak to ourselves. So, it is quite possible, and quite likely, that a person who didn't receive support as a child will feel alone and have a hard time trusting others.

If you look at the structure of this book, you will notice community is the first chapter. That is quite intentional. Surrounding yourself with people who believe in you can help you to counter-act the self-talk that says, "I am not enough," or "I do not deserve."

Safety

If you are afraid all the time, this inextricably impacts your feelings of safety. It is an unfortunate fact that many children live in homes where they do not feel safe. Then, these children grow into adults who must find a way to adjust and compensate. For some adults, this feeling of being unsafe will permeate all areas of their life. A common manifestation of feeling unsafe is putting up walls. No one can hurt you if you don't let them close, right? The problem with this is that these walls also inhibit the connection we have to our spirit and prevent it from ebbing and flowing and changing and growing as it should.

I am not suggesting that any of you put yourself in unsafe situations but simply that a little discomfort and a bit of trust can go a long way. Remember, if you want to feel love, you will inevitably have to experience moments of sorrow. It is all part of the human experience. But those moments of love make the sorrow seem less intense and more manageable.

SKILLS OF THE SPIRITUAL WARRIOR

There are other causes of spiritual dis-ease. In fact, book after book could be written about nothing else. Since this is a book is about empowering yourself, it is sufficient to have a taste of the causes. The real focus is on what you can do about it. Know from the beginning that working your way out of spiritual dis-ease will not happen overnight. It takes time and steps. This is even more reason to start now. It is possible that you are already applying some of these tools in your life, and that is fantastic. It means that on some level, you are tired of living the life you have lived. Even picking up this book is a sign that you desire something more. So let's feed that desire.

Shadow Work

The first tool I want to talk about is shadow work. One of the great gifts of spirituality is that we get the opportunity to face the shadows we tend to lock away and ignore. We all have them, things in our past we would prefer not to be there. No force nor spell nor amount of wishing can change these things. What can change is our attitudes and feelings toward our past. Our perception is what determines if we let our past control us or if we break free. Make no mistake, it doesn't happen all at once and it is not comfortable. Working on our shadows is something that happens over time. The point is not to destroy the shadows but to first acknowledge them and embrace them. Then we are able to live our lives without the shadows being in control. There is something powerful about owning your past. No matter how unpleasant it is, it is yours.

Therapy

Sometimes, there are magical things disguised in the mundane. Therapy can be one of those. There are skills learned in some therapy sessions that can absolutely be applied to the magical world and vice versa. Think about art therapy, just as an example. Art is magical. You can paint, draw, and sculpt to manifest what you desire from life. The act of speaking what is in your heart is also powerful and freeing.

Awareness of Self

Who are you? Don't tell me your name or your occupation. Who are you at your core? If you were to close your eyes and feel the energy of self, what colors would you vibrate with? If you were a song, what would be playing at your core? Who we are is not a fixed point or a solid moment. It is fluid and shifting. The nuances of who we are can vary from day-to-day and depend largely on situations and the people around us. But at the core, the truest truth of our higher self is consistent. This is the who you should be aware of.

Twelve Steps

While the concept of a twelve-step fellowship was once reserved for alcoholics, the tools (aka steps) have proven so successful that a similar model exists for everything from overeating to codependence to other forms of addiction. I am a member of a twelve-step fellowship and I have done the steps (yes, all twelve). I can tell you that step work is essentially shadow work done with the aid of a guide, and the results are amazing if you dedicate the time and energy to it. I know some of you have tried twelve-step programs in the past and have been deterred by the use of the word *god* or higher power. My experience has been that Odin and Freyja fit as well into this framework and idea as any of the other gods or the pantheons they inhabit. There is a list of several fellowships that utilize twelve-steps, or a similar format, that can be found in the resources section of this book. If one doesn't work, try another. Most of you reading this book qualify for at least one.

Meditation

Meditation is really my go-to answer for most things. Stressed? Meditate. Need insight? Meditate. Talking to the gods, healing yourself, and coping with emotions: they can all be done through meditation. So, too, can you address your shadow self.

Acts of Power

Acts of power are acts that enable you to own your power. They are acts that let you embrace your truest self. They also help you manifest your world. I think there's a tendency to see ourselves as victims of the world. When you engage in acts of power, you are essentially saying, "I am not a victim of the world. I create my own destiny." So how do you do that? What are these acts of power? Well, there are a lot of them. Frequently, they coincide with choices we make. And, when we make the one that resonates with our truest selves, despite opposition or fear, we make a choice to step into our power.

Random Acts of Kindness

This seems like something so insignificant but it's not. Think about the act of holding a door for someone. What that act says is that you value the other person enough to pause your life for a few moments to make theirs a little easier. Now, they may say thank you, they may not. This act is not about their response, it is about the act itself. It is about performing a little kindness without concern for a reward.

What this does is puts you in tune with the energy that flows through all beings. We are all connected, like it or not. The world of quantum mechanics is just beginning to see all the ways that cells and molecules interact and coincide. My suspicion though is that within a few decades' science will see that kindness to other living beings helps our own bodies resonate with kindness. This is something intuitively and instinctively known by many people. But sometimes, science is slow to catch up with instinct.

Boundaries

This is going to be a hard one for a lot of you. It was for me. There seems to be this feeling that because of what we have done or what we have been through with another that we owe them a life debt. You may owe someone, money, time, energy, an amends, etc., but this does not give them the right to ask for something that violates your boundaries. How do you even know what your boundaries are? Well, this may take some practice. If something makes you uncomfortable, that is worth looking into. Did the person touch you without consent? Did they borrow your clothes without asking? These are examples of some of the boundaries you may be tempted to write off. But don't. It does not matter if Uncle Charlie, who you have known your whole life, is the one who puts his hand on your shoulder. If it makes you uncomfortable, say something. You don't need to be rude about it (unless they keep up the behavior. You can simply say, "Please don't do that. I don't like it." Anyone who respects you will stop. Maybe your bestie wants to borrow your car but you don't want her to. Instead of just saying yes because she's your bestie, tell her no. No is okay. You are allowed to say no for any reason or no reason at all.

Advocacy

No one is going to advocate for what you need in life if you are not willing to do it first and with the most vigor you are able to give. You should be your strongest advocate. The tricky part when you are getting out of the DOC and entering back into the world is to know what those needs even are. I mean, half the time just having a job seems like the only thing that matters. And it does matter. There are slightly different rules when you are on parole versus after your sentence is over. But this doesn't mean that you can't advocate for yourself. Much of this will come in the form of picking your battles while you are on parole. Will you be able to advocate away your UAs? Probably not. But can you advocate for a curfew extension? Possibly. If you have been following the rules and proving yourself, then state your case. The worse they can do is tell you no. Learning how to present your case is a valuable skill. "For reasons x, y, and z, I should be allowed an extra hour on my curfew." This will come in handy when you ask for raises later in life. Or when you are trying to explain to a company why they should hire you despite your background.

Expression

Having an outlet is something I recommend for everyone, no matter their belief system. We all need a place, a moment, when we can be, and show, our truest selves. If you like to write, write. If you paint, paint. If you play an instrument, then play it. If you are a metal worker or singer or woodworker or anything not listed, create with the deepest part of your spirit. Do not worry about what it looks like, sounds like, or feels like to others. This is about you. The process of creating is itself a magical act. Let your voice speak through creation. This is an act of power because you are allowing a side of your spirit to awaken and be free. This act of expression is between you and the gods.

STONES FOR SPIRITUAL HEALTH

Carrying, wearing, or sleeping with stones can help you take their energetic personalities with you wherever you go. From a spiritual standpoint, they link you to the earth and any other element they represent. While a stone can't do all the work in healing your spiritual side, it can aid the work you are doing and give you an added boost. Here are some of the most well-known and accessible ones.

Opal

You can't look at opal without suspecting that is has a mystical and magical side. Opals help you align your sense of self-worth to your sense of spirit. They can help you feel your higher callings and sense of destiny. Just looking into the universe that each one seems to contain will help you realize your place in the cosmos.

Moonstone

Just as moonlight illuminates the night sky, so too does the moonstone help you to illuminate the darkest parts of yourself. Moonstones are known to help align your different energetic systems (think chakras) and bring them all into resonance and balance. Though the pull of the moon is subtle at times, it is strong enough to bring about real change and impact all life on the planet. This energy can be found in the moonstone.

Chrysocolla

Chrysocolla can help you become empowered and express yourself artistically and vocally. Its resemblance to the sea in a reminder of the safety of the womb and the crashing of the waves that deposit and pick up sediments, seaweed, and small animals to be used and recycled by Mother Nature. This churning of the waves helps keep the sea and the shore alive. Within you, this churning of ideas helps keep you alive mentally and spiritually.

Peacock Ore

The world is noisy and sometimes it is hard to hear our higher selves over the noise of the world. Peacock ore can help you drown out some of that external noise and bring you to a point where you can focus on your inner work, your spiritual rebirth.

When you hold a piece of peacock ore in your hand, it can help you overcome fear and feelings of self-deprecation.

Sapphire

If you find opposition between the mundane (physical) world and your spiritual path, a sapphire can help bring them into alignment, often boosting your intuition in the process. It can also help to clarify your thoughts and see your situation more accurately and without the negative self-talk that frequently accompanies spiritual dis-ease. This allows your view to be accurate, fair, and balanced.

Citrine

If you are working on setting and holding boundaries, then citrine is a great stone to carry with you. Its bright color helps you to be self-assured, confident, and own who you are. These qualities make it easier to feel okay with the boundary-setting process instead of holding misplaced guilt.

HERBS FOR THE SPIRIT

Growing plants is great for spiritual health. Some of these you might not be able to grow due to size, living area, or legality issues in your area, so be sure to research before you do so. As either a tea, incense, seasoning, or living plant, these herbs can add a magical boost to your spiritual workings.

> *Awakening*: gotu kola *(Centella asiatica)*, saffron *(Crocus sativus)*, elder *(Sambucus nigra)*, peppermint *(Mentha × piperita)*, hibiscus *(Hibiscus rosa-sinensis)*, willow bark *(Salix alba)*, cayenne *(Capsicum annuum)*,

eucalyptus (*Eucalyptus globulus*), and sage (*Salvia officinalis*).

Spiritual healing: calendula *(Calendula officinalis)*, lavender *(Lavandula angustifolia)*, nettle *(Urtica dioica)*, rose *(Rosa* var.*)*, rosemary *(Salvia Rosmarinus)*, hawthorn *(Crataegus monogyna)*, chamomile *(Matricaria chamomilla)*, bay *(Laurus nobilis)*, cloves *(Syzygium aromaticum)*, and marjoram *(Origanum majorana)*.

Focusing: lemongrass (*Cymbopogon citratus*), bacopa (*Bacopa monnieri)*, fennel (*Foeniculum vulgare*), rosemary *(Salvia Rosmarinus)*, ginseng (*Panax ginseng*), celery seed (*Apium graveolens*), lemon (*Citrus limon*), guarana (*Paullinia cupana*), peppermint (*Mentha* × *piperita)*, and ashwagandha (*Withania somnifera*).

Contentment/balance: ginger *(Zingiber officinale)*, peppermint *(Mentha* × *piperita)*, lemon balm *(Melissa officinalis*), danshen *(Salvia miltiorrhiza)*, St. John's wort *(Hypericum perforatum)*, chamomile (*Matricaria chamomilla*), ashwagandha (*Withania somnifera*), and damiana *(Turnera diffusa)*.

Sense of self: rose *(Rosa* var.*)*, orange *(Citrus sinensis)*, oregano (*Origanum vulgare*), hawthorn *(Crataegus monogyna)*, sage *(Salvia officinalis)*, vanilla *(Vanilla planifolia*), damiana *(Turnera diffusa)*, and oats (*Avena sativa*).

HEALING SYMBOLS

The following symbols can be used to aid in your healing process. To further expand on their meanings and uses will take a little research, but you may even find yourself recognizing these symbols in mundane usage throughout the world.

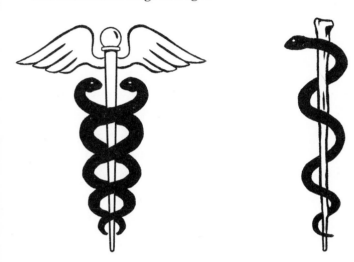

Caduceus and the Rod of Asclepius

You may recognize the caduceus for its use in the modern medical field. However, its history didn't originally have to do with medicine. The caduceus originally belonged to the Greek god Hermes, messenger of the gods. The symbol was intended to be adapted from the original rod of Aesculapius/Asclepius, which showed one snake wrapped around a rod.[17] Aesculapius is the Greek god of

---

17. M. Prakash and J. Carlton Johnny, "Things You Don't Learn in Medical School: Caduceus," *Journal of Pharmacy and Bioallied Sciences* 7 (April 2015):S49–S50, https://www.ncbi.nlm.nih.gov/pmc/articles/PMC4439707/.

healing. Over the last couple of centuries, the two symbols became mixed and intertwined (pun intended) to include two snakes.

Choku Rei

This is one of the symbols used in Reiki and is thought to be the most versatile of them. While it is not a healing symbol on its own, it does make a person more receptive to healing energy. Drawing it on the palms of your hands, and other key body centers, will help aid you as you do your spiritually healing work.

Beith

Ogham is an alphabet system that was once used ancient Ireland and Britain. Each symbol represents a tree or plant. When used in as a magical symbol, you can use the essence of the ogham to gain the properties of that tree. Beith is the birch tree. It is believed to have a protective nature and symbolize growth. It is a great symbol to utilize for spiritual healing. Beith is also the first letter of the ogham, making it appropriate to start your research with it.

Bind Runes

A bind rune is a symbol created by merging individual runes to make a single symbol with an intended purpose. The one shown above is for health. It is a combination of laguz (renewal), inguz (growth), and algiz (protection). If you look closely, you can see many more runes overlapping and merging to lend their energy to this shape. Runes come from the Old Norse tradition and can be quite versatile in their use.

Personal Symbols

Think back to a time when you were sick. Is there a specific item that made you feel better? Maybe it was a blanket, stuffed animal, statue on your nightstand, or other such item. These can be incorporated into your healing. You can either include the item itself or a representation of the item. Your teddy bear may be long gone, but the image of a teddy bear lives on in the healing iconography of your mind.

SPIRITUAL POWER

There are actions you can take daily to step into your spiritual power. Think about everything that exists within you that does not have a physical shape, volume, or container; all this undefinable and unexplainable part of you is spirit. It fills the space within and between your cells. It is you and beyond you. Spiritual power helps increase the efficiency of all your other body systems. If you are spiritually sick, you will be more prone to physical and mental sickness. Regardless of your faith, pantheon, or practice, you have a spiritual element that needs to be fed.

Talk to the Gods

Feel free to fill this in with any kind of divine entity: the goddesses or the universe. It does not matter what form your concept of the Divine takes, one or many or formless or human shaped or half animal. What is important here is to have a conversation without asking for something. Your words can express gratitude or joy or maybe you just talk about your day. Perhaps you dedicate a meditation to just getting to know your deity or give them an offering on a random Tuesday just because. My experience has shown that when I talk to them, they are more willing to talk to me.

Make Time

Time, though really a man-made concept, is very precious. It has the habit of slipping away before we even realize it for what it is. Make time for your magical practice. Make time for your serenity. Make time for feeding your spirit. Perhaps you are sitting there thinking, "I don't have time." This is a fallacy of thought. You will be surprised how much more time you seem to have when you devote five, ten, or twenty minutes a day to your spiritual welfare.

Study Nature

There is more wisdom to be found within the natural ebb and flow of nature, in her changing seasons, and in her timeless cycles then can be found anywhere else. How you study is largely up to you. Maybe you get permission to go camping for a weekend and you commune under the infinite night. Maybe you sit in a park and listen to the stories in the wind. Perhaps your nature study comes from documentaries or books or growing a garden. If you are willing and make the effort, she will teach you.

Forgive

Forgive yourself. Forgive others. Forgive situations suspended in the past. Easier said than done I'm afraid. But start small. If someone cuts you off in traffic, instead of following them for miles while riding their bumper (something I have *never* done), forgive them and understand that maybe they didn't see you or maybe they are in a hurry. You don't know and never will. So, forgive and don't give them more energy or time.

Sit in Silence

Some of you I can feel already tensing up at this prospect. That's okay. I understand. When I got out of prison, I felt so uncomfortable in my skin that I wanted the TV going while playing on my phone and listening to music. I couldn't sit with myself. Like most things, you are going to eat the elephant one bite at a time. When you wake up, give yourself five minutes before you turn on any electronics. If you accomplish this, that is a huge win. If you don't, try again tomorrow. Spiritual growth is about the process of growing, not reaching a destination overnight.

Experience the Sun and Moon

Have you ever stood outside on a sunny day and just felt the warmth of the sun? How about on a moonlit night? Have you felt the rays of the moon wash over you and bathe you in the same light that has been seen since the beginning of humanity? If you haven't, you are missing out. I would issue the additional challenge of doing one, or both, of these during different phases or seasons. Is the new moon energy different than the full moon? Is the feeling of the sun different in August versus September? If you do this, there is a good chance that you will better understand the cycle of seasons and the cycle of seasons within your body. You will come to know intuitively the subtle dance of the energy currents that impact our world and our magic.

Action

Action is arguably the most important tool in the spiritual warrior arsenal. Small actions you take now have a big payout later. Don't believe me? Well, I can tell you that I did not just go from felon to author. There were many steps in between; initiation, teaching, volunteering, more teaching, a few hundred freelance articles that don't bear my name. Then there was the actual sitting down and writing that first book. There have been hundreds of candles lit and countless prayers to my patron deities. All of this is while I was working, going to school, rebuilding relationships, and living life. If you are waiting for the right moment to take that first step, you are in that right moment, right now.

Certainly, there are other tools you can utilize to gain spiritual health, but if I gave you all the answers, assuming I even had them, then you would be deprived of the thrill of searching for them. Start with the tools above and see where you go from there. If you come across a technique that you think you should add to your spiritual warrior skill set, do it.

DARKNESS AND LIGHT

I have never met a human being who is all light or all darkness (though some people do come close), and I doubt I ever will. It is perfectly healthy to have imperfections. It is perfectly human and perfectly beautiful. If you were perfect, what motivation would you ever have to challenge yourself and to change? Right now, while you are on parole, it may be hard to see your life ever getting better or being different. But it already is different. Prison...now parole. Eventually, if you follow the rules, you will be off parole. Then what? Well, that is up to you. Decide now if you want to live your life in and out of a cell or if you want to try something different.

SHADOW SELF MEDITATION

This meditation can be triggering. It may be helpful to set a timer to tell you when to come out of the meditation or have a friend nearby to gently guide you back if it becomes too intense.

Sit or lay down comfortably. Take a few moments to focus on your breathing. Think about a moment when you did something you regret. You can start off small, it doesn't have to be the worst thing you have ever done in your life, just something you wish you could take back. Be in that moment. Try to see this experience as though you are watching from somewhere else or as someone else.

When the scene replays, ask in your mind, "What was my motivation for this?" Wait for an answer. Usually, one word or a sentence or a symbol will come into your mind. If you start to get the answer in sentences or paragraphs, then focus on your breathing to calm yourself and ask again, "What was my motivation for this?" When you get your short, simple answer, spend a moment to acknowledge that truth you have just discovered.

Replay the scene again, this time, when it is done, ask yourself "what did I learn from this?" Wait for the answer. Just as before, if you start to wander, focus on your breathing and try again. Once you get your answer, move on to the third part.

Using the answer you got from "What did I learn from this?" think about other scenarios during your life where this lesson came into play. How many times were you faced with the opportunity to make this decision or a different one? What did you choose? How will you know when this choice shows itself again?

When you are ready to return, thank yourself for taking part in this work. Then, focus on your breathing and slowly become aware of the world around you. When ready, slowly open your eyes. If you are going to keep a meditation journal, use the moments just after returning to record your experience.

When you meditate frequently, it becomes less difficult to enter and exit meditation, and you will gradually be able to enter deeper states. Be patient with yourself and the process.

SPELL TO HEAL THE SPIRITUAL WARRIOR

I wish I could give you a spell that would undo all your trauma, truly I do. While this spell doesn't exist, you can still use magic and meditation to begin the healing process. This spell works best if you are naked, or at least in your underwear. If you are not comfortable with this, for *any* reason, you can do this clothed. This is about recognizing, acknowledging, and learning to like (and eventually love) all the parts of yourself. You might find it hard at first; that is okay. You can repeat it as often as you would like.

What You Need

- A mirror big enough to sit in front of
- A comfortable chair, pillow, or cushion
- Five candles (any size) for lighting (more if needed)
- Lemon grass essential oil

Ritual

Sit in a room well lit by candles.

Get comfortable on your cushion. Gaze into the mirror in front of you. Look at each part of your body, one at a time. Start with your face. See yourself without judging what you see. Spend a few moments looking into your eyes and at your nose and at your skin. Look at all these parts of your face and say, "I see my eyes and they see me. I see my nose. I see my mouth. I see my skin. I see this face that looks back at me. This face is exactly as it should be." Dab a bit of oil on your brow.

Move on to your torso. Once again, avoid the temptation to judge what you see before you. Look at your neck, chest, shoulders, and abdomen and say, "I see my neck that holds my head up high. I see my shoulders and my chest. I see my abdomen and I see my skin. I see my body proportioned exactly right for me. This body is exactly as it should be." Dab a bit of oil on your chest.

Move on to the lower portion of your body. Look at your hips, butt, groin, legs, and feet one at a time and say, "I see my legs that carry me. I see my hips and my groin. I see my legs and I see my feet. I see my body proportioned exactly right for me. This body is exactly as it should be." Dab a bit of oil on your pelvis.

Now look into your eyes for as long as you can. While you are gazing into your eyes say, "I see who I was, who I am, and who I hope to be. I see that I am not perfect, but it's okay not to be."

Put some oil on your right fingertips. Then return your gaze to your eyes. Place the oil on your heart and say "I see that I am loved, I am worthy of love, and I can give love. My body, mind, and spirit are now connected as one."

Sit for a moment or two or five and appreciate all the parts of yourself. When you are ready to end, take a few deep breaths and touch the floor in front of you. Say, "I am me. I am me. I am me. So mote it be."

Take your time returning to the mundane world. As you snuff out each candle, thank the element fire for providing you light to see your true self. As you re-dress, notice how your clothes feel draped over your body. And, as you exit your space, do so knowing that you have begun the healing process, not finished it. It is okay to be exactly where you are.

CHAPTER 5
MAGICAL ETHICS AND LAWS

The subject of magical ethics can be a double-edged sword. On one hand, the Pagan paths are about choice and personal understanding of the gods and spirituality and such things. On the other hand, we are not free from consequences. You can, in theory, do anything you want. But freedom of choice does not equal a freedom from consequences. It is not for me to stand over you and make your choices for you. But it is appropriate, in a book such as this, to discuss different views on magical ethics. Then you can explore what makes the most sense to you, i.e., what feels true to your higher self?

You will hear terms like black magic, white magic, grey magic, chaos magic, and the like. But it is important to understand that these are human terms for something that expands beyond humanity. These terms do not apply to magic itself. They apply instead to how the person using magic is intending the outcome. The effectiveness of a spell has to do with the amount of focus you can put on the desired outcome. Everything else is pomp. Pomp has its place, but it is nothing on its own.

Keep in mind that morals and ethics in Paganism go beyond spell casting. In fact, a lot of Pagans aren't Witches and will never cast spells. Having a moral and/or ethical code is something that should expand into all areas of your life. If something gives you a feeling that it is wrong, go with that. Once you have discovered what your own moral and ethical codes are, stick to them unless you have a really good reason to challenge them.

MORALS VS. ETHICS

For a moment, let's detour and look at the difference between ethics and morality. Though the words are often interchangeably used, they are not the same thing. What is ethical can vary based on the society you live in. What is moral is something you feel is right or wrong despite the norm. One example is infanticide. In ancient Sparta it was ethical (and expected) to leave a sick or deformed child out in the wild and let nature take its course. This, of course, led to the death of the infant in almost all cases. In modern society, this is unethical and abhorrent.

Morality would be if you were a member of this ancient Spartan society and you disagreed with the practice. In such a scenario you may even have chosen to keep the child and raise it. Morally you have done nothing wrong. But ethically, you are going against the cultural norms of the society you live in.

To further complicate things, we must add legality to the mix. While ideally laws are ethical and moral, sometimes they conflict with one another. In the Spartan society example, let's say that it is illegal to raise a child that is born with a physical deformity. By keeping the child, you are breaking the law. If you have a moral compass that values the life of your child and values the laws of society, then you would be in quite the moral and ethical pickle.

The reason I am bringing this up is so you begin to think about the differences between morals, ethics, and legalities and so that you begin to question why you hold on to some of your ideas and values. I can tell you all day long "Don't do this type of magic," or

"Do _____ in certain situations." However, I'm not you. You need to make your decisions and you need to at least try to understand why you make certain choices. This is how you learn to make better ones.

PRISON ETHICS

Prisons, jails, halfway houses, and sober living spaces are all their own microcosm within a much bigger world. What was the main rule in prison? Don't snitch. That was it. Keep your head down and do your time. Now that you are out in the world again, do you want to hang on to the same toxic ideas and behaviors that helped you survive in prison? You are certainly welcome to but they won't serve you very well. A fight on the yard and a fight at the office are drastically different even though they both have consequences. On the inverse, borrowing something from someone in another unit can get you a write-up in prison. But if your coworker on the outside wants to loan you a mug, a jacket, or whatever, no one bats an eye. These examples should help illustrate why you should not carry your prison ethics into the real world.

How to Break DOC mentality

So how do you do it? How do you untrain and retrain yourself so that those things you did when locked up don't trickle out? You do it slowly. You have patience with yourself. And you accept that you are not going to be perfect at it. I'm going to give you some tricks that worked for me with the hope that they will work for you, too.

Explore Spirituality

Most of you, I am willing to bet, know you believe in something but don't know what. That's okay. Here's why: You don't have to have all the answers, you'll never have all the answers. And you can change your mind anytime. Start somewhere, anywhere. Maybe you used to love Egyptian myths as a child. So, pick up a book on Egyptian mythology or watch a documentary on the practices. Maybe you'll love it all or none of it or maybe a piece here and there. Then you decide, do you want to learn more about Egypt? Was there a particular god you were drawn to? Maybe you are done with Egypt now, but you saw a book on shamanism. Go there next.

One of the biggest mistakes we make as humans is thinking that we must pick one thing and stick with it forever. You don't. While you are searching, let yourself be guided. The Kybalion, Spiral Dance, tarot, mysticism, shamanism, and the *Eddas*, immerse yourself in all of it. You will learn what it feels like when you hit the piece that resonates with your spiritual truth. Keep that. Then be flexible if it later changes. Many adults are searching for something, though most don't know what. Many will hang onto what they were taught as children and never dare to ask why. If you picked up this book, perhaps those beliefs given to your child self no longer suit you. Search and keep searching until you find "it," whatever "it" may be.

Ask Why

Kids ask why. They ask it a lot. It is this uninhibited curiosity that feeds their craving to know the intimate details of the world and to understand it. As we grow into adults, asking why is discouraged. We are told to just accept things. Just get a job and get married and have babies. But why? What if you are meant to write a novel or travel or become a stage magician? Why aren't you doing these things? Ask why you believe certain things? Why do you believe certain things about yourself?

Let me clarify. While you are on parole, get a job and do the things that are required of you. Do those things so that you can get off paper and start doing some of the things your spirit is begging you to do. Not only should you ask why, ask what you are meant to do and how you can achieve that. Yes, felonies will provide a challenge. But few things are impossible if you are willing to put in the effort to achieve them.

Meditation

Meditation unites the body, mind, and spirit in a way few other things can. In a meditative state, you can ask questions to the Divine, you can work with your child self, you can create new worlds. The potential for meditation might be limitless. If you are inexperienced, that's okay. Do a little search for "meditations for _____." You will probably find one. Anything from healing your inner child to meditations for stress or to help your body heal. Since I discuss meditation in other places, I am not going to go into too many details in this section. Simply know that it helps, it really helps.

Ask Ancestors / Spirits for Assistance

Throughout time, countless cultures have practiced ancestor veneration and/or worship. Many cultures still do, though the dates of observance and the methods used vary by culture. Though ancestor veneration is not as prevalent in the western world, we do still see it in the celebrations of Samhain, Halloween, Día de los Muertos, and All Saints Day. You can get in touch with your own ancestors through methods. These may be biological ancestors, such as your grandparent's grandparent or they may be cultural. To contact your ancestors, you can opt to pray, meditate, dance a dance handed down to you, or put an item that meant something to them on your altar. Your ancestors (usually) have a vested interest in your safety and success. When you ask for their guidance, offer them goods or a service.

Accurately Check Yourself

When we are kids, we tend to be more open to learning things that conflict with what we believe. Let's say that as child you believed that all dogs were males and all cats were females (yes, I had a phase where I believed this). Now, along the way I learned that this was not true. When I learned this, it did not challenge my sense of self. I welcomed the new information. However, it gets me wondering how many things did I carry into adulthood that I believed to be true but weren't? Things like I was not good enough on my own, so I needed to have a spouse or significant other in my life. Or that I was allergic to onions when really I had a bad one many years ago and stopped eating them but being "allergic" gave me justification. (as if I needed to justify why I ordered my food without them). You may have grown up believing all kinds of things that aren't true, just like I did. When was the last time you asked yourself, "Is that true?" "Why do I believe this?" "How do I know this is true?" Also, be careful not to confuse thoughts, beliefs, and facts.

Here is a thought exercise that will get those synapses firing. The color I think is blue and the color you think is blue; are these the same color? We may all agree that a certain cup is blue, but how would we know we all perceive it to be the same color? If you believe it to be green, perceive it as green, does that make your perception correct and everyone else's incorrect? Or are both then correct?

Have Realistic Expectations

If you spend your whole life from this point on trying to only be positive all the time, you will be doing yourself a disservice. Sadness is a real emotion; feel it. Anger is real; give yourself an outlet for it. If something bad happens to you, you do not have to pretend to be okay with it. Something I have seen time and again is a person, or people, who will try to avoid feeling emotions that aren't pleasant. Some will bury their emotions and avoid acknowledging them, covering them with a smiling face and a mantra of "Everything is fine." You have probably heard people talk about not feeding your anger. This is true. But you shouldn't stuff it down and ignore it. If you are trying to be all love and light, you are going to miss out on some of the growth that comes from pain and sadness. It is unpleasant but necessary. To know day, you must know night. To know happiness, you must know sorrow.

Retrain Your Brain

All these tips and all this advice is utterly worthless if you do not put the effort of consciousness behind it. Though this sounds complicated, it is simple (in idea though not always in practice). What this means is that when you become aware of a thought, action, or behavior that is damaging, you notice it and make the effort to change it. Maybe you think, "I want to hang out with my friends. My friends always hang out at the bar. I'll go to the bar." Problem is, on parole this could land you back in prison. If that's your goal, go right ahead. If it's not your goal, you can choose to not go, ask your friends to meet somewhere else, or go somewhere else and meet some new people. If you choose the latter, try out this evocation to the minor Greek goddess (some say spirit) Philotes.

You can hold a daisy in your hand for while you chant, for an extra boost.

> Philotes, Philotes, friendly Philotes,
> I call on you now to show me.
> Philotes, Philotes, grab my hand.
> Guide me to friendship of the truest brand.
> Philotes, Philotes, be at my side.
> Aide me in expanding my circle, be my truest guide.

If you used a daisy while chanting, place this flower outside as an offering to Philotes.

WELL-KNOWN MORAL/ETHICAL CODES

Since the very beginning of written history, mankind has tried to institute moral and ethical codes. Some were created to help human beings coexist harmoniously in the society they lived in. Some were created at the whims of leaders to establish hierarchy and control. Others have been made to help enforce cultural norms or to tap into humanity's innate need to create order in a sometimes chaotic world. It is interesting to consider that most people follow the ethics of their society without ever wondering why. As you look at the ethical and moral codes below, try to view them not just in the context of your society but in the context of the society that created them.

Chivalry Code

This is essentially the code that the European knights of the Middles Ages were to follow. Though it is heavily influenced by Christianity, there are some tenants that could easily apply to any faith. The idea was to balance the two sides of their nature. I won't cover all of them here, but I do want to look at the ones that tend to fit well within Pagan principles.

> *Seek wonders:* You should always pay attention to the wonders in life. There is magic all around you. We attract what we focus on. If you're always open to the wonders of the world, you are more apt to see them.

> *Do not attack one another:* Other people who are going through things are not your enemy. Read that again. And again. If you are struggling to feed your family, then the other person who is struggling to feed theirs is not your enemy. They should be your ally. If there is someone doing well on parole and you are struggling, then instead of wishing them ill, learn from them. As a species, we have been divided by politics and media and race and religion, and the list goes on and on. But all of this is surface level. Two people wanting to better their lives should not be in opposition. We have been led to believe that there is only so much to go around. In reality, a small percentage of the population controls more than their share of the assets. To regain the assets we are due, we need to unite, not divide.

> *When called upon, defend the rights of the weak with all your strength:* Remember this one for now or for years down the road. There is likely to be a time when you are called to defend someone who can't defend themselves or who can but is vastly

outnumbered. What will this look like? It's hard to say. But it could come in the form of defending someone who is being bullied. It could be saying "Hey, maybe we should give that person a job even though they have a criminal background." It could be signing petitions or going to rallies. It could come in the form of a vote for something you believe in, even if your family/friends disagree. Or maybe, when a group of people is standing around mocking someone, you tell them that you refuse to take part. Sometimes the first one to speak up against something unjust is the one who gives others permission to do the same.[18]

Wiccan Codes

Understand that not all Pagans are Wiccan. Wicca is new revival of magical and earth-centered practices, and it is fairly modern. Wicca is a beautiful faith, and it is also how many people are first introduced to Paganism. Even if you are not Wiccan, you can utilize some of the tenants found in Wiccan for your own moral code. These are some of the commonly used moral guidelines.

> *Law of three:* In a nutshell, it explains that whatever you send into the universe, you get back. If you are miserable and nasty to people and animals, then this is what your experience in this life will largely consist of. It should not be interpreted to mean that if you are always nice that only good

18. Mike Greenfield, "Knight's Honour Code of Chivalry," Widjiitiwin, September 8, 2017, https://widjiitiwin.ca/knights-honour-code-of-chivalry/.

things will happen to you but being overall genuine and true to your highest self does come with its own rewards. The reason it is times three is because your actions affect you on a mental, emotional, and spiritual level.

An it harm none, do what ye will: This statement attests to the freedom found in Wicca. You are free to be who you are—any race, sexual identity, gender, if you like to host sock puppet theater on the weekends or if you have an affinity for naming different types of cabbage, that's all fine. *Be* who you are as long as it harms no one, including yourself. Let's look a little deeper at this, shall we?

My interpretation is intentional harm or doing something that has the likelihood of causing harm. If you race matchbox cars and one flies off the track and whacks somebody in the face, did you cause harm? Yes. Did you intend to cause harm? I should hope not. Do you have to stop racing matchbox cars? No. But you do have an obligation to put in practical measures to help prevent it in the future.

Let's look at a trickier scenario. Say you come from a very conservative religious family who does not approve of your Pagan faith or some other aspect of your life. They might even say that this aspect of yourself is causing them harm. In this case, be true to you. Because denying who you really are does more harm in the long run than just placating those who don't approve. I'm not saying you must blatantly go out of your way to make them uncomfortable (please don't). But maybe learning a bit of acceptance is part of their life path.

Balance: Nothing stands alone. Not one thing. There must be an ebb and flow of the tides and a shift in the changing seasons. You may live some place where these shifts and changes aren't as evident, but they exist, nonetheless. When you make a choice, you are adding to either the ebb or the flow. When you did the crimes that landed you in prison, you put out an energy into the world and shifted it. Now, you are in a place where nothing from the past can be undone. The die has been cast and paths laid out. Interestingly though, you can help to restore the balance, which is not always perfectly aligned but instead fluctuates. Earlier I said that if you want your life to change, you must change your life. Start by restoring your balance. If you used to steal, then make it a point to pay a fair price for what you need. If you used to use people for drugs or sex, then get to know some people just to know them without wanting these things in return. If you used to cheat on tests, then push yourself to study harder. You get the idea.

Virtue Theory

This moral code states that each person should try to act like other virtuous people, meaning you should try to perform right actions at the right times and in the right way. This sounds simple until you start asking who decides what a "right" action is anyway? The Greek philosopher Aristotle would say that humans are naturally geared toward virtuous actions and that if these actions are not in excess, then it's fine. We have all been brought up with social cues that are generally accepted. Think about emails or text messages that you would send to your best friend versus. a person you are trying to date. Or that feeling of embarrassment when the waiter says, "Enjoy your meal," and you respond with "You too." These are the kinds of things Aristotle was referring to. And, for the most part, they are so socially ingrained that we don't even have to think about them.

Here's the problem though. If you've been incarcerated for a long time, these social cues haven't been practiced. There is going to be a learning curve. Also, a lot of us who have been to jail and/or prison may not have adapted those social cues in the first place. Dysfunctional families and years of doing drugs don't exactly help a person develop the best social skills. How, then, are we to know what is virtuous? And what do we do when we find ourselves in those awkward situations? Making friends was hard for me when I got out of prison. Sometimes it still is. I felt like my DOC number was emblazoned on my head and that is all that people would care about. For a while, I didn't tell people. I didn't lie about it but it was not on my top-ten-fun-facts-about-me list.

The advice I can give is two parts. First, be patient with yourself. You have been through a lot. People who haven't been to prison or suffered abuse or lived in a drugged-out daze, well-meaning as they may be, will not completely understand. That's okay. It is my greatest wish that no one ever must understand these things … ever. And I'm truly sorry that you do. So, while you reintegrate into society, don't beat yourself up anytime you do something awkward. It will happen, move on. Second, hang around supportive people. Believe it or not, there are a lot of people who have left prison and gone on to lead incredible lives. You don't have to hang out with the same three people who you always get into trouble with just because you fear social awkwardness.

Hammurabi's Code

I am including a section on Hammurabi's code because it clearly illustrates that what is legal or ethical in a society is not always moral. Hammurabi was the ruler of Babylon from 1792 to 1750 BCE. He is remembered because he is responsible for one of the first written law codes that we still have record of today. How it was compiled is interesting because it chronicles the court decisions of the time and uses these as a basis for the law code. Keep in mind this was before the days of due process, appeals, and innocent until proven guilty. What is the result? Well, let's just say that you did not want to break any laws in Babylon. Probably the most well-known of Hammurabi's 282 laws is 196, which reads: "If a man put out the eye of another man, his eye shall be put out."[19] This is where we get the expression "an eye for an eye." But, keep in mind that this will make the whole world blind.

The laws go on in a similar fashion. If you accused someone of a crime but can't prove it, you'd be put to death (law 3). If you broke into a house to steal, you'd be put to death and buried at that house (law 21). A woman who served one of the many gods of Babylon could not open a tavern or enter one to drink. If she violated the law, punishment was—you guessed it—death (law 110). These are some pretty harsh laws, but completely ethical for the time.

---

19. L.W. King, trans., "The Code of Hammurabi," The Avalon Project: Code of Hammurabi, Yale Law School, last updated 2008, https://avalon.law.yale.edu/ancient/hamframe.asp.

The Ten Commandments

I can feel some of you flinching at reading this phrase. Isn't this a book on Paganism? Yes, it is. When you study belief systems that are not your own, you not only expand your mind but you start to see the similarities that exist. When you remove people's interpretations of the Bible and Christianity, and look at the teachings on their own, there are some good guidelines that exist. Notice I said *guidelines*, not *rules*. If you don't believe me, I'll show you. Commandment three: "Remember to keep the sabbath day holy." From this one, you could deduce that you should take a day off, not be a work-a-holic, and take time for self-care. You are sacred. You are holy. Therefore, devote a day to honoring yourself as the holy vessel you are.

Commandment seven: "Thou shall not steal." Pay your way. That's good advice. Nature exists in a balance, an endless cycle of give and take. So, take but also give. Commandment five: "Thou shall not murder." This doesn't mean you can't defend yourself; it means you don't take a life frivolously. Some of you reading this may like to hunt or fish. This then can be applied to mean eat what you kill and don't just kill for the sake of killing. My point here is not to persuade you to use the Bible. It is to get you to think beyond the surface level and to understand and challenge your own belief systems.

Physics

Okay, you've got me. Physics is neither a code of ethics nor a basis for morality. So, what is it doing here? Well, one of the things that has always attracted me to the various branches of Pagan practice is the level at which they collaborate and overlap with scientific principles. I am not a physicist, but I do find physics fascinating. In fact, there is much within physics and quantum physics that could explain the "how" of magic. This possibility excites me to no end. Here I will present a brief overview of some physics principles that apply well to the magical and Pagan worlds.

> *Principle of Relativity*: In a nutshell, this means that the laws of physics apply to everyone no matter where they are or what they are doing. The universe is not picking on you. The same laws that govern you govern everyone else on the planet. If something is amiss in your world, look at the actions and intent you are putting into the world. Is there a scientific principle that you are going against or fighting? Perhaps the reason you are unsuccessful on one path is because you are meant to be walking another.

> *First Rule of Motion*: An object will remain in a state of rest or moving at a constant speed until it is acted upon by something else. For our purposes, this means that you will remain on the current course of your life until you make changes or until changes are made for you. The latter is usually legal intervention—jail, prison, court ordered rehab. But *you* can be the force that changes the trajectory of your life. You can get a better job. You can make the most out of court ordered classes. You can go back to school. You can resolve differences with family. You can make small steps that change the course of you (the object in motion).

Second Rule of Motion: The rate of change to the momentum of an object over time is directly proportional to the force applied and will occur in the same direction. I don't want you to think of force in this context as trying to open a stuck pickle jar. Instead, I want you to think of it as finesse, effort, and energy. The more work you put into changing your life, the more change you will see. The second part speaks to directionality. If you are putting your effort into manipulating, cheating, lying, and stealing, this is the outcome you are pushing toward. Here's a hint: these never have good outcomes in the long run. On the other hand, if your effort is going toward proactive and prosocial activities, then you are pushing your life toward receiving things that are proactive and prosocial. Please don't let prosocial scare you. This does not mean you have to conform and fit into a bubble. You can still be you and live within the world.

Third Rule of Motion: Every action that occurs in nature has an equal and opposite reaction. There is going to be a tendency here to hear "opposite" and go into either/or, black-and-white, good vs. bad thinking. That is not what opposite means. It is more like tension. If you stretch a rubber band, you are pulling on the band, but the band is also pulling against your fingers. That is what opposite means. Looking at how this applies to life and magic: we have the equal reaction where if you pick up a penny, you have a penny. If you light a candle and do a spell, there is a reaction. If you light a candle and do a spell every day for a week, you get a bigger reaction. If you spend thirty minutes in meditation visualizing your outcome each day you light that candle, you get an even bigger reaction. When you stretch the rubber band to its limits, it will either snap or you'll let go. Either way, that stored energy is released. So too with magic there is a point, often called a cone of power, where magic is stored, built up, and released, just like that rubber band.

Metaphysics: Magic does not exist on just a physical plane. It is too big and too encompassing to be so limited by the physical. It is comprised of time, space, and energy. We too, exist on multiple planes of existence. When thinking of time though, this is not man's limited view of time where seconds bleed into minutes which gather into hours. The gods do not know "Next Tuesday at 3 p.m." The closest they come is to the timing of the phases of the moon and the turning of the wheel. When you want something to manifest quickly, say something akin to "Without hassle or delay." Time, when you are looking at it universally, is not linear. This means that all moments which ever have or ever will occur exist at the same point. Try not to get too overwhelmed by this idea. I bring it up only to illustrate that your definition of time and the universal definition of time vary greatly.

Space, too, is much larger than we could ever comprehend. On a dark night, far from where the city lights overtake the stars, it is possible to look up and get a sense of just how small we are in the grand scheme of things. Magic exists in every star and every space between. It is fun to think that maybe, on some other planet, there are alien equivalents of Pagans who dance around bonfires on a night lit up by two full moons. When we perform magic, we are connected to them as well as ourselves. Matter, on a quantum level, can go from one spot to another without travelling through the space between.[20] This is a possible explanation for how Reiki or distance healing work. It could also explain how a spell done in Bethesda could impact someone in Sydney in real time. In alternate planes, we can breathe under water and reshape mountains with ease. The alternate planes of existence are just as real as the clothes you are wearing.

There is a phrase some of you will be familiar with: "As above, so below. As within, so without." Our physical body is not separate from our minds nor our spirit. We are not separate from the animals and the trees and the stars and the planets. They are part of us and we are part of them.

---

20. Andrew Zimmerman Jones, "How Quantum Physics Explains the Invisible Universe," ThoughtCo, August 16, 2019, https://www.thoughtco.com/quantum-physics-overview-2699370.

> What happens to us on a microcosmic level effects the macrocosmic level and vice versa. When you drink enough water, it can be felt in your cells. When you get a hug from a loved one you have not seen in weeks, it vibrates through your body. Nothing stands alone. We are all tied together in a web of intrinsic detail. Your actions matter.

If this last section appealed to you, then I suggest you read the *Dancing Wu Li Masters* by Gary Zukav. I have included the information under the recommended reading section of this book. Some of the concepts presented within changed my worldview. But like anything else, use what applies and scrap the rest.

BIRTH, DEATH, AND REBIRTH

Many of the beliefs that you have concerning birth, death, and rebirth are based on the ethics of the society and environment in which you were raised. Let's briefly look at some of the ethical and moral issues that arise from these concepts and those that influence them.

Prior to Birth

Prior to birth, we choose what lessons we need to learn in the upcoming incarnation. It is my belief that those who have the toughest of lives are those who have lived many lives before. The simpler lessons have been learned in previous incarnations, so we must then move onto the harder ones. It is like going from kindergarten to first grade, the work gets a bit more challenging. This is not to say that everybody doesn't go through struggles, because everyone does, nor should you use this as an excuse to compare your life to the lives of others. The point is simply that we are all in different stages of our spiritual evolution. If you have gone through trauma in your life, then perhaps it is because you are ready to learn the tougher lessons.

Make no mistake though, not everyone learns the lessons they are meant to. One unchangeable rule of nature is that we will repeat lessons until we learn from them. Maybe it takes one lifetime, maybe it takes many lifetimes. Think about how this could apply to your own life. If you are reading this, you have made mistakes. Not because this is a book for Pagans who are on parole, but because we have all made mistakes. What did you learn from those mistakes? What are the gods trying to get you to learn still? On the grand karmic scale, if you keep dating the same type of person and keep going to jail because of how you spend your time with this type of person, there's a big hint about the lesson you are supposed to learn. It is up to you to take notice and do something about it. If you want change in your life, you must change your life.

Life

What makes something alive? Does life lie in a beating heart? In sentience? Or is there an as-of-yet unidentifiable spark that makes something alive? The philosophical discussions around this topic have been going for centuries. The truth, is we may never know; it could be Mother Nature's most widely guarded secret. Regardless of what makes you alive, you have life. And what you do with that life can shape your present and your future. Not just in this life but the next. And although we have other lives, this one still matters. Not just for its effect on the future but for its own sake.

What does this have to do with ethics? Well, there are a lot of things that happen in life that change how we view the world. Someone who is a parent may have different views around what constitutes ethical or what is a priority than one who is not. Think about occupational differences. In the medical field, doctors take the Hippocratic oath to uphold certain ethical standards for their field. One of these is to treat the sick to the best of their ability. Someone who is not in the medical field will have a different set of guidelines. Education level, life experiences, exposure to other cultures, incarceration, books that have been read, TV shows watched, income level, and the quality of one's support system are just some of the influencing factors that help shape a person's ethics and morals.

It is important to point out, though, that you don't have to personally experience something, or have it impact you, to care about it. One example is wanting everyone to make a living wage. If you make a good living and can support your family, you should want the same for everyone else. We live in a society where, culturally, we are trained to see people as either for us or against us. But this is not reality. The world is not either/or, for/against, you/me; it exists in varying shades between the extremes. I hope you will remember this, not just on parole but after.

Note to PO:

It is my hope that you will apply those last four sentences into your interaction with people on parole. I know you have a job and parolees don't always make it easy, but try to remember that some of them really do want to make the right choice. They need guidance in "the how." They are not your enemy any more than you are theirs. Mental health issues, substance use disorders, codependency, and lack of support coupled with the monetary and physical challenges of being on parole do not help set them up for success.

Death

We are going to take a moment and broach a subject that brings up so many emotions: death. Most people are quite uncomfortable speaking about death, as if talking about death makes it real and ignoring it makes it an illusion. Others are intrigued and fearless in talking about death. The passing of a loved one will undoubtedly bring up moral and ethical questions for you regarding how to honor them. This especially comes up if you are Pagan and they are another faith, particularly one that was not accepting of yours. Here's what I can tell you: Nothing you do will inhibit or hinder their process into the next life. You are not that powerful. The best advice I can give is to grieve and allow yourself to feel. If you need to light a candle for them to get closure, do it. If you want to go to their very conservative funeral, do it. Want to make an ancestor altar and put their picture on it? Okay, do so.

Sometimes, when a person dies, if our identity was interwoven or defined by theirs, then their death can feel like a death of self. I can't speak for what works for everyone, but I can tell you that letting yourself grieve will look different for each of you. If the person who has passed had a big impact on your life, but that impact was negative, I would encourage you to forgive them. This is a big ask, I know. But if you manage it, even if you take the first steps to forgiving them, you will feel better. And I've included a spell to get you started.

Forgive the Dead Spell

Once someone passes over, they begin the healing process of their spirit. Nothing you do or don't do can interfere with their process. What can be affected is your emotions towards the individual that has passed on. If someone crossed over leaving you with unfinished issues, this spell can be used to help you forgive them and grant yourself some peace.

What You Need

- Pen and paper
- Black candle, carved with deceased person's name
- Matches or lighter
- Five tealight candles in any color (Make sure you have a container or stand for each one so they don't burn furniture)
- A fire safe bowl
- Salt water (you can add three pinches of salt to a regular cup of water)

Preparation

Saturday night is a good time to do this spell.

Arrange the five candles around the outside of your working space in a circle. Place the black candle on your altar or in the center of the circle.

You will want to spend a few days making a list of what this person did. Try to avoid writing paragraphs. The spell works best when this list is concise. It might read, "Leaving me at the mall when I was two, not coming to my recital, denouncing me when I came out of the broom closet, etc." This is your list, and no one is ever going to see it. There might be some dark stuff on this list. Please reach out for support from a therapist, trusted friend, or sponsor if it gets to be too much. You can always leave the darker items off and come back to them after time has passed.

Spell

Start at the door and sprinkle the salt water around the room. Say, "May this space be cleansed in the name ____(deity)____."

Light the candles in the circle one at a time. As you light each one say, "Let this light illuminate my heart and keep me safe."

Now face your black candle and pull out the piece of paper you have written on, say, "____(deity)____, for the healing of my heart and mind I seek to forgive ____(Deceased person)____for these things I see as crimes."

Light the candle. One by one read each thing on your list and say, "I forgive you." For example: "____(Deceased person)_ Grandma___, ____(what they did) leaving me alone____, I forgive you now and forever more." Take a few deep breaths in and out before you move onto the next one. If you find yourself wanting to cry, do so. You are in a safe space.

When you have made it through everything on your list, use the flame of the black candle to light the paper and put it into the firesafe bowl. Let it burn to ash, relighting it if necessary.

Let the black candle burn down. Sit in the circle until you feel the spell has worked, then thank the gods/goddesses for attending. Take the tealights and put at least one in the rooms of your house where you spend a lot of time or keep them in your room if you are unable to put them in other rooms.

Make sure to eat nutritious food afterward.

Rebirth

Not all Pagans believe in reincarnation. While it is a common belief, there are other views of the afterlife. I'm talking about reincarnation here because it is a common belief among many Pagans and because it is what I believe. In fact, I think the different views of the afterlife explain places where our spirits hang out and do what they need to do to prepare for the next life. For those that do believe in reincarnation, there is usually the question of do we always come back as human, or do we come back as other animals? To assume that humans are the highest life form attainable is an anthropocentric viewpoint. One which every cat on the planet would disagree with. Perhaps there is a level of sentience that a species must obtain? Or perhaps our spirit's molecules dissipate and filter and become parts of many other creatures. I wish I had answer for you, truly I do. But because I don't you get to think about these concepts and how they fit into your view of the world. If we really are all a part of one another how does this change your interactions with people to whom you are indifferent? Favorable? Unfavorable?

DESIGNING YOUR OWN MORAL CODE

So, now you've got all this information. All these examples of morality and ethics. And mental exercises to get your brain thinking. How do you know what to follow? This is for you to figure out. The process will involve getting to know who you are and what you value. Which is more important freedom or loyalty? Social acceptance or being true to yourself? Change or comfort? Raising your kids or feeding your ego? Where do these things differ and where do they follow the same path? Do your actions reflect these values? It is easy to say where you stand it is harder to live by it.

Much of this will involve change and evolution of thought and learning. Things that matter to you so much today may be insignificant in a year. That is a good thing. Think of yourself as a lake. If you have a fresh source of water (knowledge, growth, the Divine, adaptation, etc.), then you will stay ever moving and full of life. If you remove that source, then you stagnate and become mucky.

You can help keep the river flowing by being your most authentic self, which is what we'll discuss next.

BEING YOUR MOST AUTHENTIC SELF

It's hard to be human. Here we are, these spiritual beings, these energetic bodies contained in mortal shells that are trying to grow all the while knowing that growth doesn't feel good while it's happening. The good news about this is that once you accept that you are an energetic body, not a physical one, you can begin to alter your perception of the world around you. Don't like something? Change it. Don't like prison? Stop making choices that get you there. Are you angry all the time? Take up meditation, yoga, and/or tai chi.

When you are living in tune with your most authentic self, you will attract that which supports you and repel that which doesn't. I find that my most authentic self communicates through this feeling of peace and contentment. When I am anxious about a decision, I play a scenario in my head where I made a different choice or completed a separate action. When I get to the one that I am supposed to follow, I lose my anxiousness. While learning to live within your most authentic self will be quicker for some than others, the important part is that you begin the journey. With that in mind, I'm giving you a spell to help you get started.

ELEMENTS OF AUTHENTIC SELF MEDITATION

This meditation is a movement meditation. If you are restricted in the movements you can do, then substitute the "walking" part of the meditation with something that is better suited to your abilities. The important part is to let yourself be present in nature. It is helpful to leave your phone and electronics in your car or to at least have them on silent/off and in the bottom of a bag where you won't be tempted to look at them.

What You Need

- Any accessible natural space

Meditation

Go to the natural space of your choosing. When you get there, take a deep breath. Look at the place you have chosen. Take just a few moments to consider if this is your ideal natural space. Do you wish it was by the sea? In the mountains? Or is it the place you feel most content?

Begin to walk. While you walk chant:

> The wild out here, the wild in me.
> Who I am and who I'll be.
> All these elements speak to me, speak to me.
> Let me know what you see, what you see.

Keep chanting and walking until you find yourself in a spot that feels like it is where you should be. Sit there, under the trees, upon the rocks, near the stream, wherever it may be. Repeat the chant again, but this time, on the last line say, "Elements tell me what you see when you look at me." And, let the elements tell you what they see. You will want to listen with extra senses. This can include putting your hands in the dirt, holding a stone, feeling the wind on your skin, and smelling the world around you. There may be a feeling or a knowing or a scent that comes to you. It is in all these ways, and more, that the elements speak. But you must be still to hear it.

Spend time here. Give this moment, the one you are in, the focus and attention it deserves. When you feel you have received the insight you need, you may begin your journey back. Do not rush. Let this journey out of the woods be intentional. Let it be a conscious awakening back into who you are.

AUTHENTIC SELF SPELL

What You Need

- Images, pictures, or drawings of things that represent 1) who you used to be 2) who you are now and 3) who you want to be. For example, you could go through a magazine and tear out images of people dressed in the height of fashion, motorcycles, leather boots, paisley prints, a random blue square that calls to you, a telescope, and others. There really isn't a wrong way to do this, you are looking for images that speak to you, even if you don't know why.

- Your favorite picture of yourself (make a copy if you don't want to damage the original)

- Four candles: three white and one that is your favorite color

- One yellow glass candle representing the Celtic sun goddess Étaín who oversees transformation

- Sunflower oil

- Food and drink to offer the goddess

- An offering plate and cup

Spell

Place the food and drink in their receptacles and set them on the altar or off to the side.

Arrange the three white candles in a triangle, with your favorite-colored candle in the center.

Take a moment to separate the images that represent you.

Around the candle to the left place the images that represent who you used to be.

Around the candle to the right place the images that represent who you are now.

Around the candle at the top place the images that represent who you want to be.

Place the picture of yourself under the center candle.

Place the yellow candle above the triangle. Rub a few drops of sunflower oil on the candle. And say,

> Étaín, goddess, shining one,
>
> glowing goddess of the sun,
>
> I ask you here to guide me now
>
> In finding my most authentic self."

Light the candle and say, "Welcome Étaín." Now bring your attention to the candle on the left. This candle represents who you used to be. Look at the images that surround it. Feel their energy. When you feel compelled to, say any words that come to mind about these images. What does your past represent to you?

Light the wick and say,

> The place I was, no longer am I.
>
> That place was needed at that time.
>
> I release that which tied me down
>
> And keep the things that build my foundation sound.
>
> The lessons learned they shall survive
>
> But I free myself to my new life.

Sit and watch the flame dance for a few moments. Notice any feelings you get. Then move on to the next candle.

Now bring your attention to the candle on the right. This candle represents who you are now. Look at the images that surround it. Feel their energy. When you feel compelled to, say any words that come to mind about these images. What does your present life status represent to you?

Light the wick and say,

> The place I am, a sacred moment I abide
> A culmination of the moments of my life.
> I release that which ties me down
> And keep the things that build my foundation sound.
> The lessons learned they shall survive
> But I free myself to my new life.

Sit and watch the flame dance for a few moments. Notice any feelings you get. Then move on to the next candle.

Now bring your attention to the candle at the top. This candle represents who you want to be. Look at the images that surround it. Feel their energy. When you feel compelled to, say any words that come to mind about these images. What does your future mean to you?

Light the wick and say,

> The place I see, my truest me.
> Is the place I'll need it to be.
> By releasing that which tied me down
> I have built my foundation sound.
> The lessons learned they shall survive
> I free myself into my new life.

Sit and watch the flame dance for a few moments. Notice any feelings you get. Then move on to the center candle.

Hold the picture of yourself in front of your eyes for a moment. Try not to judge any of your features. Just see your face as it is, acknowledge and accept it.

Place the photo of yourself at the base of the center candle and take a few deep breaths.

Starting at the left candle, visualize a blue cord extending from the left candle to the center candle. Say, "My past is part of me."

Then go to the candle on the right, once again visualize a blue cord wrapping itself around the center candle. Say, "My present is part of me."

Then go to the candle at the top and again visualize the blue cord wrapping around the center candle. Say,

> My future is part of me. Goddess Étaín! You have now seen these parts of me. These pieces of me. Help me put them together. Help me make them fit. Help me to become whole and true to my most authentic self!" Sit in the sacred space for as long as you need to before moving on to the next part.

Hold up the drink to the Goddess and say, "This drink I offer to thee. As I sip it, I take the energy of the sun into me." Drink some of the beverage and set the cup down.

Next hold up the food and say, "This food I offer to thee. As I bite it, I take the nourishing rays of the sun into me." Take a couple bites and set the rest down.

"Goddess Étaín, I thank you for joining me. I thank you for guiding me. I thank you for your wisdom. This rite is now done. I invite you to stay or go as you deem appropriate. Hail and farewell." Snuff out her candle. You can use it next time you work with her or any sun deity.

Take a few deep breaths. Then, bring your attention to the room you are in or the world outside of this ritual. "I am now ready to rejoin the world. To complete the everyday things which must be done."

Exit the space and eat some food to make sure you are grounded.

Make sure that the candles you have left burning are in a place where it is safe to do so.

Let the offerings for the Goddess stay on your altar until morning or until the candles burn out. Then take them outside. And say "For the Goddess" as you pour the drink out and leave the food for her furry children.

CHAPTER 6
TOOLS AND RITUAL ITEMS

Now that you are out of prison, you can start collecting more tools if your living situation allows it. For those of you in a halfway house or in community corrections, have some patience. You will not be forbidden from being Pagan because you don't have an athame or thirty-five different types of incense. Remember, all the tools you could ever need are within you. Having tools is just an added fun. There is a certain pageantry that comes from putting on your cloak and stepping into a candle-lit room and calling on the gods or ancestors to join you.

If you are anything like me, you will have this urge to go collect as many tools as you can in the next day or two! Your excitement is great but not always the most wallet friendly. Especially considering that you have rent, treatment fees, UAs, court fines, and many other expenses. The gods will not shun you for putting food in your belly before buying tools. With this in mind, we're going to look at some the more affordable tools first then look at the pricier ones.

When I was on parole, I did about an 80/20 split. That is 80 percent of my tools budget went toward candles, herbs, oils, and other things that I would need to buy again. Then 20 percent went towards the things I could use over and over, such as my cauldron, mortar and pestle, and the altar itself. This meant that it took me a while to collect everything I wanted. But it also meant that instead of having to buy a cheaper wand I didn't really like, I saved up for a while and got to splurge on a really beautiful one. However you decide to collect your tools, just make sure it makes sense to you, your needs, and your budget. For several months, I did all my spell work with little more than a few candles and an altar. Since your altar is your working space, we will look at that first.

ALTAR

As mentioned previously, your altar is your working space. In the most basic sense, it is a table, but it's connection to the mundane ends there. It is the place where your tools are held and it creates a place where you and the gods and goddesses, ancestors, elements, or other astral beings can meet and exist in the same space. There are several different types of altars, and they serve several purposes. Regardless of the type of altar you have, know that it is not some stagnant thing. Your altar reflects your magical world and the status of your life at any given point. If your altar is well tended, so too will your life be.

Creating a Space

Depending on where you reside, the rules which are in place, and your own level of comfort with being "out of the broom closet," you may want either a permanent altar (one you don't take down) or a temporary one which can be stored, tucked away, and hidden when it is not in use. Once you decide which option you want, at least for now, then comes the fun part, setting it up.

It is traditional to have your altar in the east, to connect to the rising sun, or north, the element of earth, in your space. However, if you have a bedroom with a west-facing window and you want that window to be part of your altar setup so you can catch moonlight, then put it there. There are some methods which are traditional, and some things which are universal laws, and others that are a matter of preference. But if you have a reason behind what you do and it makes sense to you, then it will add more to your magical and spiritual practices than doing something because you were told to. Intention is key.

While your altar can be made from anything, natural materials tend to work best as they provide a direct link to nature. Some of the most common and customary woods to use are oak, ash, and hawthorn. I have also seen some beautiful stone, glass, and driftwood altars that are true works of art. You want to be sure that whatever you are using, it is designated as a sacred space. This means that you coffee mugs, TV remotes, and other mundane items, stay well away.

Now, what if you can't have or don't want a permanent altar for whatever reason? Well, it is perfectly acceptable to keep some ritual items in a box and set up your altar each time. There may be a shoe box or a plastic tub which holds all your ritual items. Then you can use this container as the altar itself or use a piece of wood as your altar. Either of these can be dressed up with a cloth, paint, symbols, anything you desire. One added benefit is the mobility. It is easier to take a portable altar to the park, for example, than it would be to take a full-sized altar.

Another option is to not have an altar at all. Despite what you may have heard, there is no tool which is required for you to practice magic nor to have rituals. If you are in a halfway house or a treatment center, there are other things for you to worry about than having an altar. You can still feed your spiritual side regardless of your living situation. Just don't let yourself believe you can only do so if you have tools x, y, and z.

Why Have One?

Having an altar serves many magical purposes, not the least of which is to provide a place to practice and to commune with the gods. Having an altar, especially one where you will see it every day, reminds you to take time for your spiritual practice. We all need this reminder sometimes, especially as days turn into weeks and the cycle of seasons fades one into another. It is important to stop, slow down, and make time to commune with the gods.

An altar is also a designated magical workspace. So, consider this, if you are learning something new, and you have a set place that you go to when it is time to study, then your brain prepares you to study when you enter that space. Having an altar works the same way, but with magic. Each time you stand before your altar, your body, mind, and spirit shift to help you be prepared for the working you are about to undertake. It becomes familiar, comfortable, and alluring, especially after some time. This effect can also be achieved with a temporary altar. Each time you set it up, you are sending out those energetic cues that it is time to practice.

Arguably the most important purpose of the altar is to serve as a point of focus for spiritual or religious practice. When I touch my altar, I can feel it hum with all the magics of rituals past. Every candle I have burned on it, every knot tied in front of her, every rune read, or card drawn, or chant spoken, is remembered by my altar. This is why she is my focal point. I know when I stand in front of my altar that it is time to let the magic of the universe flow through me.

Different Types of Altars

In this section, I want to discuss the difference between an altar and a shrine. Though the words are often used interchangeably, they are different. An altar is your ritual working space and shrine is an area erected to honor a deity, person, or idea. An altar is for worship; a shrine is for remembrance. The space with your athame is your altar. A bookshelf set up to honor Hecate or your grandmother is a shrine. You can have a prosperity shrine or a prosperity altar (or both). For now, try not to get too hung up on semantics. Just know that there is technically a difference between an altar and a shrine, and that while you can have more than one of each, most people only have one working altar.

Generic Altar

When I say generic, I don't mean that your altar must be boring. I simply mean that if you have limited experience in setting up an altar, this is a guideline of what that would look like. It is traditional to place your altar along the north or eastern wall of your space. If you can't use one of these directions, don't worry. You can set up your altar where you have room and treat it as "magical north" instead of directional north. This just means you act as if this is east for the purpose of your spell casting.

Once you have decided where to put your altar, now is the time to decide what to put on it. Once again, these are what you would traditionally find on an altar. As you expand your practice you will develop a sense for what you like and what you don't. Assuming your altar is along the north wall (or magical north), when you are facing it the "top" would be north, to your right would be east, closest to you is south, and on your left-hand west. In each of these directions, you'll put representation of the element that corresponds to each direction. I've given you a few examples to give you an idea. You can pick one or two from each column and your elements will be covered.

- North/earth: bowl of salt, stone(s), bowl of earth, green candle, or a pentagram.
- East/air: feather, incense, yellow stone, essential oil, or a wand.
- South/fire: candle, red stone, lava rock, cinnamon stick, or an athame.
- West/water: bowl of water, blue stone, mirror, moonstone, or a cauldron.

Then, you'll want your working tools, such as your wand, working candle, and cauldron if they are not already on your altar. If you have the room, include a representation of the God and Goddess you work with mostly (your patron), or those who you will be calling on for the spell. Then, I recommend adding seasonal items, like pinecones in the winter or sunflowers in the summer. You can adjust, add, and place the items to suit your own aesthetic preferences.

> Note to PO:
> When you enter the home of a Pagan individual on parole, please be mindful that the altar is sacred. Room and house searches may be routine but to touch the altar of a Pagan parolee is akin to desecrating a crucifix or other religious iconography. If you absolutely must search the area on and around the altar, ask the person to whom it belongs to pick up the items and allow you to look (not touch) them.

Generic Shrine

There are many different types of shrines you can erect. If you don't know what kind of shrine you want to keep, that is okay.

You can start by setting aside a space where you want your shrine to be. Physically clean the space first with a dust rag. Then, clean it magically. You can do this by doing a smoke cleansing around the area then visualizing the area filling with a beautiful, clean, light. If you can't do a smoke cleansing, anoint the area with a few drops of essential oil; clary sage, rosemary, or lavender work well for this.

There is probably one item, perhaps a stone or a picture, that inspired you to create this shrine. Set that item up in the space first. Next, you will want to use your intuition and your extra "clair" senses. More information on "clair" senses is available in *Paganism for Prisoners: Connecting to the Magic Within*. Ask the item, "What would you like to have accompany you?" Then listen for a moment. Do you get a feeling or see an image? This is the answer to your question. The image or feeling may be so subtle at first that you find yourself questioning if it is accurate. Trust yourself and add the next item. Repeat this process of asking, listening, and placing until you feel that your shrine is complete.

Prosperity Shrine

Please don't limit yourself to thinking prosperity only means money. Yes, it can be financial prosperity, but you can be prosperous in your work life, spiritual life, romantic life, creative life, and in so many areas. Having a prosperity shrine is essentially having a permanent or semi-permanent space dedicated to drawing prosperity into all areas into your life. You can decorate with green, mint, and money for financial prosperity. For prosperous relationships (friendships), you can decorate with yellow, sunflowers, and olive branches. To be prosperous in your family life, include pictures of loved ones, tokens that remind you of happy times, and lilac or hyacinth.

Ancestor Shrine

Ancestor veneration goes back tens of thousands of years with archaeological evidence showing signs of it happening in the Neolithic era (FYI, I'm a huge history nerd).[21] Cultures all over the world have believed that our ancestors stay with us and watch over us long after they pass. This tradition is so strong that many modern cultures still practice ancestor veneration and worship. You can create a shrine for one or many ancestors. Good items to use are pictures or paintings, personal items that belonged to your ancestors, black altar cloths, black candles, incense, skulls, grave-yard dirt, and the like.

Deity Shrine

Is there a specific god or goddess that has spoken to you since you were a child? Or maybe one that has recently gotten your atten-tion? Setting up a shrine is an appropriate way to thank them for their attention. In this case, the colors and items you use should be specific to that deity. For example, an owl would be appropriate for the Greek goddess Athena. Then, you might go with white or yellow as colors to have on your shrine and handmade crafts as offerings to this goddess.

Animal Shrine

If there is an animal whose energy you want to have manifest in your life, having a shrine for them is an excellent way to do that. Dragons carry the ability to roar (aka speak their truth) and are very protective. Let's say you want this powerful and elusive

---

21. "Religion 101: Ancestor Worship in Ancient Europe and the Arctic," Daily Kos, April 0, 2019, https://www.dailykos.com/stories/2019/4/3 /1847528/-Religion-101-Ancestor-Worship-in-Ancient-Europe-and-the -Arctic.

dragon magic in your life. You could have a dragon representation in picture or statue form. Then, depending on the dragon, some brown or green candles, dragons blood incense, stones, and rocks, etc. I make it a habit to "feed" my dragons regularly by anointing a candle and lighting it for them.

These should give you an idea of the kinds of altars and shrines you can set up (provided you have the time and space). They should speak to who you are and what you are trying to achieve. Try not to worry about whether you are doing it "right." Focus instead on how it feels.

Etiquette

Your altar is not just some stagnate thing that takes up space. Your altar has personality and life and carries the memory of all the rituals you have done upon it. Remember that your altar is sacred space. There are some guidelines that are good to follow when it comes to etiquette and respecting your altar.

- Clean it regularly: A great time to do this is each new moon when there is the energy of new beginnings. Set a reminder in your phone on the new moons to give your altar a cleaning. You don't need to get too fancy; a wipe down and a new altar cloth make quite the difference.

- Magical/spiritual items only: Your altar is a sacred space and should be treated accordingly. It is no place for your car keys, soda cans, TV remotes, etc. Let the mundane objects stay in the mundane world.

- Don't let others touch: People love to touch magical items. They are drawn to them from their most primal place. However, when people are touching your altar, or the items upon it, they are putting their energy into it. Even if they have good energy, it is not your energy. So set that boundary and ask that people not touch your altar. Think of it this way. If someone had a classic car, it would be disrespectful to just walk up and touch it and start adjusting the mirrors. The same idea applies to your altar and your tools. With a group altar, members of the group use and decide what to put on the altar.

Candles

Candles are great because you can use them for anything. They can represent God and Goddess, serving in place of statues. They can be inscribed with sacred symbols and send out intention as they burn down. They can serve as an energy source or a focal point. They are sensual and create an ambience that is truly other-worldly. A white candle is basically a magical blank slate because white can be substituted for any color and a candle can be given any intent. Candles are also great if you live in a place where you can't be out of the broom closet: "Don't mind me, I'm just burning this innocent little candle."

Color Associations

While you could use nothing but white candles and have quite the success in your magical endeavors, there are color associations that can give your spell work an extra oomph. Magic works on energy and vibration; ideally you want to have as many items as possible of your spell work to be on the same vibration, at least when you are starting off.

White

Besides being a universal color that can be substituted for any other color, white has its own associations. It is the color of renewal and beginnings. It represents purity of intent, thought, and spirit. Use this candle color to cleanse and purify your thoughts, your intentions, your mind, or your body.

Black

There will inevitably be some people who try to tell you that black candles are "evil" or bad. Don't believe this for a second! What black candles are for is banishing unwanted energies and for instilling protection. They are good to light if you are doing shadow work or deeper meditations. Night and day are two sides of the same coin, so too are black and white candles.

Red

Fiery passion is at the essence of the red candle. It is sometimes associated with love, but more accurately, sexuality, lusty desire, and fervent love are the realms of red. Red is strong and boisterous. It is the primal sexuality, untamed and wild. It is useful to ignite the fire and start momentum. Think of it like striking a match and throwing it into a stack of kindling. The kindling is the endeavor that you want to undertake.

Orange

This is the color, and the fragrance, of mental stimulation. Orange candle are great to burn if you need help studying for a test or undertaking a creative project. It can also increase your self-confidence, particularly if you are about to present a project, idea, or creative venture. To get an extra boost, put a couple drops of orange essential oil on your candle before lighting it.

Yellow

Yellow, particularly bright yellow, is a happy color. It is great for when you need some sunshine in your life. Because it is one of the colors that represents the sun, it can also bring abundance into your life. If you are trying to strengthen friendships, use a nice pastel yellow. Carve a flower, like a daisy, onto the candle and light the wick on a Sunday.

Green

Green is the earth, her trees and plants, physical goods, and the color of paper money in the US. Because this color corresponds to Mother Earth, it houses the energy of her fertility. Like the yellow candle, green is for abundance, but more for the abundance that comes from the growth of things over time. If you are starting a business, the green candle is like planting a seed for you to nurture.

Pink

This color, like red, also represents love, but the much more tender and gentler type of love. This is intimacy, connection, love for self and love which is not romantic in nature. If you are wanting to work on increasing familial love, pink candles can help with this. For self-love spells (who couldn't use a little self-love?), carve your name on a pink candle. Anoint it with rose essential oil and say three times, "I am as I am. I be who I be. All sides of myself, I am worthy." Then light the wick.

Blue

Communication is one of my favorite skills to work on. Blue is the color of communication and clarity. If you are wanting to increase your vocabulary, for example, burn a blue candle while you learn new words. If you tend to feel anxious, pick a light blue candle and a lavender oil to anoint it.

Purple

Purple, particularly dark purple, is the color of royalty. If you want to work on your confidence, carrying yourself as though you are royalty, then purple is a great color candle to use. It is also linked to intuition and extrasensory senses, such as clairvoyance, clairaudience, and others. Our intuition is never wrong, we just sometimes choose not to listen to it. Purple can help you hear and learn to trust this voice which lives within us all.

Silver

When I think of silver, I immediately think of the shimmering full moon, especially when reflecting upon the sea. Silver is good for intuitive magic, working within the shadows of yourself and making all that which is unknown, known. Silver candles are flow and enchantment and the sacred feminine.

Gold

If silver represents the moon, then gold in invariably the sun, with all its warmth and brightness. Gold is also connected with monetary gain because, well, it's gold. When you need to bask in your own light, gold candles. Gold candles are vibrancy and action and the sacred masculine.

Candle Preparation

Now that you have picked your candle color, it is time to carve it and anoint it with oil. You don't have to do both things. Sometimes I just anoint my candles and sometimes I carve and anoint. I will say that I tend to feel a stronger magical connection when

I do both steps. But I have had some very effective spells happen without carving my candles.

Carving

If you are going to carve your candles, carve before you anoint your candle. This is a practical because once you coat your candle in oil, that oil will get everywhere. You can carve your candles with a lot of things, a pin, your nail, a coffin nail, a candle carving tool or your boline, a specially designated knife, but avoid the urge to use your athame, a ritual knife. Both will be discussed in detail later in the chapter.

How to Anoint

To anoint means to coat or rub with oil in a sacred way. How you do this is going to depend largely on the type of candle you are anointing. Tapers, the tall thin ones, you anoint from wick to the middle of the candle, then from the base of the candle to the middle. This gives a magical boost when this center is reached. Votive candles, the wide, medium height ones, I usually anoint with a line of oil around the middle.

For tealights and glass candles, tip the oil onto your finger and rub it in a circular motion to put the oil on the top of your candle. You can also use a pin to poke a couple holes into the glass candles, this puts your oil in the candle versus on it.

Athame

An athame is the ritual knife, usually double edge and traditionally with a black handle. It is never used to cut anything physical, but instead will be used to cast circle, perform the cakes and ale rite and direct energy. It is a powerful tool, there is just one problem:

your parole/probation officer may (and probably will) veto you having one and any halfway house is *definitely* going to tell you no.

Let's get real for a moment, because I know at least some of you are thinking, "I just won't tell them." This is the kind of thought I would have had back in the day. This is a mistake. First, if they find it, you could lose your freedom. But more importantly, this is a time in your life when you will be challenged to decide the path you will walk. In the beginning of this book, I talk about you being at the crossroads. The road you will go down will depend on the choices you make. So, even if you are sure that it wouldn't be found in a room search you are reinforcing those sneaky, manipulative, and dishonest behaviors that invariably contributed to incarceration. If you want to do something different, then you must *do* something different.

Now that this spiel is out of the way, let's look at some of the options you do have. The first is you could elect to use a wand. Wands, which will be discussed in full next, are amazing and come in so many different styles. You can get them in copper, wood, stone, and can even make your own. In communal living situations, you can also use your first and second finger to direct energy.

Let's say you are not in communal living; this gives you more options for an athame substitute. You can designate a butter knife. This is one of the simplest methods. Pick a butter knife and make it your athame pro tempore. You can also check with the rules of your parole and see if there is length limit. Perhaps you are allowed to carry a pocket-knife in your state as long as it is under a certain length. There is nothing that says you can't have a two-inch long athame. You can get fancy and do the full athame dedication if you'd like. Remember: something is magical when you make it that way.

There is another option, which will have mixed results. You can go to your PO and let them see that you are genuine in your faith and make a case for why you should be allowed to have an athame. The worst they can do is tell you no. Then you thank them for their time. But what if they say yes? How good would that feel to be able to have this ritual tool, and have it in writing that you can have it, without having to worry about going to back to prison over it?

> Note to PO:
>
> For the parole officers who may pick up this book and read it to gain a better understanding of the Pagans on your caseload, I would encourage to not give an automatic no but instead honestly consider their request. Has the person asking come to you with sincerity? Have they been abiding by all the steps that parole requires? Are they nearing the end of their parole? Take these things into account. After all, a large crucifix could just as easily be a weapon and few Christians have ever been denied their access to one.

Athame Consecration

If you are either granted permission to have an athame or off paper, you can pick an athame that appeals to you and follow the steps for its consecration. This is a two-part ritual, with the first part taking place three days before the second part. Keep this in mind when preparing your start date.

Moon Cycle: Waning

What You Need

- Athame
- Black candle
- Lighter or matches

- Chalice with water
- Dragon's blood incense
- Lodestone or magnet
- Potted plant or safe dirt location outside
- Oil or paint or pen and paper
- Cauldron (optional)

Ritual

If you have an altar, stand in front of your altar as you perform the next few steps. If you don't have an altar, at least make sure that the working space is clean and free of debris and befits a magical working.

Part One

Take a deep breath and light the candle. Then light the incense. See the swirl of smoke dance into the air.

Holding your athame with open palms, pass it through the incense smoke and say,

> *Blade of steel I conjure thee,*
> *To ban such things as named by me.*
> *And as my word*
> *So mote it be.*

Take lodestone or magnet and gently stroke from blade point to hilt. Do not press hard enough to scratch the blade. A gentle passing is sufficient. Say,

> *Blade of steel*
> *I conjure thee.*
> *Attract all things as named by me.*
> *And as my word*
> *So mote it be.*

Plunge the athame into the ground outside or into the pot of dirt. Leave it there for three days and three nights. Snuff out the black candle.

Part Two

On the third night, pull the athame out of the earth. Relight your candle. You will now put the following symbols on your blade, which are symbols that were handed down to me upon the consecration of my own athame:

There are three ways you can choose to do this. Pick one.

1. You can inscribe them onto the blade with a metal carving tool.
2. You can draw them on with ink, oil, or nail polish.
3. Or you can draw the symbols on paper and burn it. Then rub the ashes onto the blade while you visualize the symbols attaching to your athame.

After you have put the symbols onto your blade, let the symbols dry before continuing to the next step.

You will then hold the blade of your chalice in the candle flame for a few moments. You don't want it to get red hot, just a bit warm. Then plunge it into the chalice of water to cool it. Do this a total of three times, each time with intent.

At the end, hold up your blade to the gods and say,

> *Blessed be thou knife of art.*

Your athame is now a sacred tool.

Please note that if your athame is not metal and is instead stone, glass, or wood you can put it near the fire instead of in the fire to avoid it cracking, burning, or breaking.

WAND

A wand has many purposes that are similar to an athame, but in a way they are less forceful and can be more appropriate for some situations. An athame is a fire tool and a wand is airy and light. Think about if you are working with the sidhe (fae) who have an aversion to certain metals, especially iron. It would be rude to have that metal waiting for them. There are some Witches who will not dip a metal blade into a chalice when performing a cakes and ale rite because they see it as putting metal into the womb of the Goddess. On this note, you may find that pointing a blade at your ancestors or deities is rude. You may even want to use a wand instead of an athame because it feels better to you or because it is less of a hassle while on parole. In any of these situations, it is perfectly acceptable to use a wand.

There are some beautifully crafted wands that are covered in stones and inscriptions or made from copper, but at its most basic level, a wand is a branch that is used for magical purposes. This means that while there are some very expensive wands, a wand doesn't have to cost you anything. If you decide to make your wand or use a simple branch, you will want to either choose one from the ground or get permission from the tree before cutting its branch. If you do the latter, provide an offering, a gift of thanks to the tree.

A wand is used to direct energy. While you were growing up, did you ever hear that it is rude to point? Well, your pointer finger is also a rudimentary wand. When you point, you are directing energy. If you are mad when you point, you are directing angry energy at the person or object you are pointing at. For certain people, especially those in tune with their empathetic nature, they can really feel the impact of this.

Wand Creation

Later in this chapter, I talk about the ways you can find/buy tools. But here I am going to give you some guidelines for making a wand. A wand is a great first tool to make because you can get quite creative with it. Ideally, it should be about the length from your elbow to the tip of your middle finger. Try out some sticks this length and see how they feel. You may want to go shorter or longer. The length should feel like an extension of your own hand.

As previously mentioned, fallen branches are preferable to cutting a new a branch off a tree. If you find a branch you absolutely must have, ask the tree if you can have that branch. How will you know its answer? You listen for it of course. Not with your ears, but with your extra senses, your clair- senses.[22] The response can be as subtle as having a sudden sense of peace or as obvious as having a leaf fall and land on you. If it is a no, you will get feelings of being unsettled or uneasy or anxious. If you get a yes, cut the branch and leave some honey or aloe (make sure they're real not imitation) on the cut. Then leave an offering and say "Thank you" to the tree.

Now that you have your wand, decorate it with runes or ogham or stones, really anything that speaks to you. If you are painting your wand, you can mix herbs and oils into the paint to add magic to it. There is also a practice called bunting. Bunting involves filling a hole in your wand with herbs and stones, stuffing the rest with wool or other natural material, and sealing the hole with wax. This

22. See *Paganism for Prisoners: Connecting to the Magic Within.*

infuses your wand with the energy of the herbs and stones. Once you have created your wand, it is time to consecrate it.

WAND CONSECRATION

For the wand consecration, we are going to tap into the planetary energy of Mercury. When you blend the incense for this spell, you can use herbs, oils, or both. Herbs should be dried. If you are using essential oils, a drop or two is all you need. The number five has associations with the planet Mercury, so five herbs or oils will be selected. You will use some for burning and the rest will mix with an oil or paint to mark symbols on your wand.

What You Need

- Mercury herbs or oils
- Mercury herbs for incense

Use any five of the following for your incense / oil and to mix with your paint or oil. Grind the herbs you will mix with the oil until they are fine.

- Clove
- Star anise
- Almond
- Cassia
- Lavender
- Lemongrass
- Thyme
- Caraway
- Dill
- Frankincense

- Peppermint
- Fennel
- Lemon verbena
- Jasmine
- Oil or paint to draw on symbols
- Oil to consecrate; any of the ones listed previously are fine
- A taper or chime candle, burnt umber, dark red, or burnt orange in color

Direction

Light your incense. Sit for a few moments while the incense smoke wafts in front of you. Think about what your wand means to you and what it will be used for. Think about the process that went into making your wand, the time it took, the meditative moments that occurred, and the time that was invested into the details of its creation.

Light your candle and say, "Mercury, hail and welcome."

Take some of the finely ground incense blend and hold it in your hand. Focus on the god Mercury, lord of communication.

Say, "Mercury, messenger, communicator, guardian of shops, bless this blend, give it voice."

Next hold up the oil, paint, or ink that you will be using to draw the symbols on your wand.

"Oil (paint) so fair, I bid you to welcome the element air."

Mix the two together, gently. Using the motion of a summer breeze not the violent shaking of a tornado.

Set your wand in front of you with the tip pointing to the left. Starting at the base of your wand and working towards the tip, draw the following symbol, which was handed down to me when my own athame was consecrated:

ꙄꙘ⊞ꙕꙄꙅꙭ·ꙅꙄꙄꙑ

With most tools, you would now asperge them. This means to magically cleanse with salt water. You will not do this with the wand. Instead, you will take your other oil and seal each end of the wand with an equal-armed cross.

Then say, "Wand you are now sacred and created. I give you life, I give you voice. God Mercury is imbued in thee. As this is my will, so mote it be."

Store your wand in a place that is worthy of its sacred status: on your altar, in a fine bag, wrapped in silk, someplace where it will be protected. If you use your wand regularly, you will develop a rapport with it.

CAULDRON

To be "cauldron born" is a term I first heard in a song many years ago. Symbolic of the womb, the cauldron has given life in more ways than one. It has provided sustenance as a cooking pot. It has provided an inky black background for divination. It has even held the fires and ashes on spells in the making. Now historically, a family only owned one cauldron unless they were wealthy. It would have been a massive pot, the iconic image of a big black pot over a fire. Now in the modern era, we have greater access to cast iron, and it is far more affordable.

When it comes time to buy a cauldron, you can find some beautiful ones online. However, if you are wanting to take it easy on your wallet, you can look for a cast iron cooking pot or a cast iron bean pot. You do not need a huge cauldron; any size will suffice. Symbolically, one with three-legs represents the Triple Goddess and one with four-legs represents the elements.

Wells

Cauldrons and chalices discussed in the next section, have a link to old European wells. With wells, there is a transformational element and a belief that they transport one to another world. Water on its own holds the power of transformation, when it in contained within the circular shape of a well it becomes the womb, it becomes a symbol of continuous renewal and change. Wells also bring forth water, which as we all know, are necessary for life.

There are countless wells in Europe, some natural and some manmade. The Chalice Well (the Red Spring) and the White Spring in Somerset, England, are among the best known. They have been in use since the Paleolithic era, though the actual well is believed to have been built by the Druids.[23] These sites are also linked to Avalon, the resting place of King Arthur. St. Brigid's Well in Clare, Ireland, is another famous well. The goddess Brighid, and her sisters of the same name, are connected to higher consciousness, higher learning, and the higher ground. Her wells, but particularly the one in Clare, are widely believed to have healing powers. In Rome, there is Lacus Juturnae, dedicated to the Roman Juturna, goddess of wells, springs, and fountains. Juturna has multiple bodies of water associated with her (all the waters in Latium). Her well waters were used in most of the Roman rituals.[24]

23. "A Brief History of Chalice Well," Chalice Well Trust, accessed August 19, 2022, https://www.chalicewell.org.uk/our-history/a-brief-history-of-chalice-well/; London Toolkit, ed., "Glastonbury Chalice Well, White Spring & Wearyall Hill," Visiting Glastonbury Chalice Well, White Spring & Wearyall Hill, accessed May 28, 2021, https://www.londontoolkit.com/whattodo/glastonbury_chalice_well.htm.

24. "Juturna," Encyclopedia Mythica, March 3, 1997, https://pantheon.org/articles/j/juturna.html.

And who could forget the wells of Yggdrasil? In Scandinavian mythology, the worlds are held up by Yggdrasil, the world tree. There are three sacred wells at the base of Yggdrasil. First is Mímisbrunnr (Mímir's Well), which is probably the best known. Next is Urðarbrunnr, the well of fate. And lastly, Hvergelmir (Roaring Kettle). This is the well that houses the monster Níðhöggr who gnaws on Yggdrasil's roots.

These are just some of the wells found throughout Europe that have history, tradition, legend, and magic attached to them. Just from the brief descriptions given here, you should be able to get a sense for the different energies you can bring forward with your cauldron and chalice. If you want to drink in wisdom, declare that your chalice will represent Mímisbrunnr and as you drink, drink in wisdom. If you want to heal someone, then make it known that your cauldron is representing Brigid's well and burn petitions or brew a broth for your spell.

Seasoning Your Cauldron

If your cauldron is cast iron, as most but not all are, you will want to either buy one that is pre-seasoned or season it yourself. You will want to periodically re-season your cast iron, just as part of the care. This keeps it from rusting and increases the longevity of your cauldron.

Start by scrubbing your cauldron with hot, soapy water. As you scrub, visualize a blue light cleaning away and removing any old energy.

Next, you will want to dry your cauldron completely. The way I like to do this is by wiping it with a towel, then putting it on the stove and leaving it there until all the water evaporates away. Once all the water has evaporated, let it cool.

Line your oven with foil and preheat it to 375°. Lining the oven will make later clean up easier.

For this next step, you can use vegetable oil or shortening. Spread a layer on the outside and inside of your cauldron. If your cauldron has a lid, coat this too.

When you have covered it completely, place it *upside down,* and bake it for an hour. Let it cool. Your cauldron should now be black in color. If it is still grey, season it again.

When it reaches inky black that is so iconic for cauldrons, take a dab of your favorite oil and at three points along the rim draw a sacred symbol. A pentagram is an appropriate symbol to use. Then say, "Thou are dedicated to the Goddess."

CHALICE

The chalice may look like a cup, but it is so much more. Within the chalice we find the representation of the womb…life giving and powerful. When filled with water, it is a potent portent to another world. The chalice connects us to ancestral mothers. And it does not matter what gender you are or identify with, you can still connect to the long line of mothers that helped birth you into existence. There is a lot of shared symbolism between the chalice and the cauldron. Where they vary is that you tend to drink from a chalice and either burn or brew things in your cauldron.

Your chalice may be any material that you choose. I would advise against silver and pewter however because they can change the chemical composition of some drinks. Silver will also tarnish rather quickly. My primary chalice is earthenware because it is sturdy. But any natural material that appeals to you is appropriate. If your living situation doesn't allow you to have tools, you can always dedicate a glass in the kitchen to serve as your chalice.

It should also be noted that some Pagans may prefer a drinking horn. This is common in Heathen practices. For the animal conscious, plastic drinking horns do exist, as do wooden cups. Most of these will come down to personal preference and what your living situation allows.

BESOM

A Witch's broom sounds almost cliché. But quite frequently things that are idiomatic have a foundation in fact. There are stories about people in Europe jumping up and down with a broom between their legs to encourage the fields to grow. This was a form of sympathetic magic, essentially showing the crops how tall to become, the higher you can jump, the taller your crops. That's the thought anyway.

The broom, often called a besom, is made up of two primary parts; the shaft, which represents the sacred masculine and the brush which represents the sacred feminine. The whole of the broom is, therefore, the joining of sacred masculine and sacred feminine energies. Try to think beyond the limitations of biological sex with this description. After all, we all have elements of feminine and masculine within us.

The besom you get can be full size, handheld, or any size in between. A besom is not the same thing as broom you get from the store. Besoms are wood-handled, often hand-made, and are not used to sweep the dirt from your floor. Instead, they are used to sweep the energy out of your ritual space, they do this without ever physically touching the floor. When you store your besom, store it straw up.

BOLINE/BOLLINE

The boline is not as similar to the athame as one might think. While both are blades, the boline is used to cut herbs, carve candles, cut physical cords, and other things which occur on the physical plane. While a black handle is traditional for an athame, a white handle is traditional for a boline. This does not mean that you cannot use any type of handle which appeals to you. The important part is that it is easy for you to tell your athame and boline apart in a candlelit room. Some beautiful bolines are shaped like a sickle in honor of either the Horned God or the crescent moon.

Your PO is likely to give you the same response they gave you regarding your athame. If you are denied permission, it is okay. You can grind herbs with a mortar and pestle. You can harvest herbs with a kitchen knife. You can even buy a special tool called a candle carver to, well, carve your candles obviously.

OTHER ITEMS

The list of magical tools you could have could go on and on and on. Those listed previously are some of the most common ones to get you started. As you develop your own practice you will get a feel for what tools you want to use regularly and which ones you don't. As you branch out, and get comfortable in your practice, you can start collecting other ritual items like the ones listed below.

Ink and Quill

When you write something by hand, instead of typing it, you put an extra bit of your own energy into it. While technically you don't need to write your petitions with a quill and ink, it is fun. And it does help you channel that old magic.

Book of Shadows

This is a book (or binder) where you keep rituals, spells, corre-spondences, etc. Traditionally, you will handwrite it, but there is no reason you can't have a backup of your book saved digitally. I like using a three-ring binder so I can organize and reorganize chapters as needed. As you start to find your niche, you may find it helpful to have a book dedicated to Celtic rituals and practices, for example.

Mortar and Pestle

A mortar and pestle are good tools for grinding herbs. But I can't stress enough how handy an electric coffee grinder will be. There are some incense ingredients that will take forever to grind by hand especially if they are stems, resins, or seeds. For other things, focus on your intension for the herbs while you grind them.

Offering Plate or Bowl

Just like it sounds, this is a plate or bowl where you put the offer-ings of food and drink you make. If you have an outdoor space, you can bypass the offering bowl and just put the offerings directly on the ground.

Divination Device

You'll want to get comfortable using at least on form of divina-tion. Now, that can be tarot, oracle cards, runes, ogham, lenor-mand cards, scrying, pendulum whatever type calls to you. But the guidance they can provide is invaluable.

Stones

There are so many of us who spent our childhoods, and probably adulthoods, bringing home rocks because "it is a nice rock." This is the same type of mindset to have when you get stones to bring home from stores. You will hear them speaking without words. They will call to you and give you the feeling that they are the stone you need.

WHERE TO FIND TOOLS

My first tarot deck ever was one I found at a thrift store. I had asked the Goddess a few weeks earlier to help me find a deck and I went about my day-to-day business. I happened to be in a thrift store, I can't remember what I was getting, but hanging in a bag, I saw a deck of tarot cards. I asked one of the store employees if I could count the deck to ensure they were all there and they went home with me that day. Since then, I have found many tools at the thrift store. The trick is that I look with my intuition, not my physical eyes. I make my intention known that I am looking for a specific type of tool. Then, I forget about it and trust that they right tool will find me. It has never failed.

Thrift Stores

I highly recommend that you do a cleansing of anything you bring home from the thrift store. Even if it doesn't have negative energy attached to it, it has energy which is not yours. While you won't be able to find everything you need there, it is a good starting point.

Craft Fairs

Buying from local artisans support your community and helps you to find beautiful, unique pieces. Buying from small shops may cost a little more, but the reward is getting an item that was created with love and, therefore, one that will have a special essence to it.

Online

Many of the artisans you meet at craft fairs also have online shops. Then there are others on sites like Etsy. If you are using a shop you are unfamiliar with, do yourself a favor and read some of the reviews. I have found cauldrons, ritual gear, and many other items from shops I wouldn't have known about if not for their online stores.

Metaphysical Stores

Many years ago, metaphysical stores were fewer and farther between. Now, there are many, especially if you live in well populated areas. They won't always say "metaphysical store," sometimes they will be listed as rock shops, new age stores, unique gifts, or other such monikers.

Create Them

Before the industrial era, everything was handmade. Some items are easier to make than others, but handmade items are inherently powerful. If you can make it, try to make it. Creating a working tool from scratch will ensure that you have a connection with it.

AN IMPORTANT REMINDER

The tools you need will come to you when they are meant to. Trusting the gods and trusting yourself are two very difficult lessons, but ones which you should make every effort to learn. As always, remember that there is no tool or number of stones or collection of herbs can take the place of having a personal relationship with the Divine. There is no symbol which serves as a replacement for faith and for action. Standing naked in a field, you have all the tools you could ever need. YOU are the magic.

When you come across a tool that you can't afford, let it go and know that it is not meant for you. Do not steal your tools! It is disrespectful to the craftsperson, the tools, and, most importantly, to yourself. Some people will let you barter, others won't, respect their decision. Magic and the tools you use to complete your work are sacred. To treat them as anything less than that is to mock the energies, magics, and forces that flow through our world.

CHAPTER 7
BASICS OF PRACTICE

The faiths and spiritual practices that fall under the umbrella of Paganism are not those well suited to paying lip service. This means that it is not sufficient to show up on the full moons and spend the rest of your time being a jerk, littering, or desecrating the earth. I am Pagan with every breath that I take. When I am not in ritual, I am still a Witch and conduct myself as one. I don't do it perfectly, neither will you. We're not meant to be perfect nor do perfect things. But being aware of your actions, their consequences, and the fact that you are not the only person on the planet who matters goes a long way towards spiritual growth.

Magic, Wicca, Witchcraft, and Paganism are all incredibly personal. This means that to a large degree "if it works, use it" applies. However, there are many things that are done because they are either historically significant, are time tested, have been handed down by others, or for a myriad of other reasons. Look at it like this. When you are new (a neophyte, a seeker) it is like you are learning an instrument. Your instructor may have you play the same set of scales over and over. They may have you learn the best way to hold your instrument. Once you get good at these things, then if you want to hold your instrument a different way or play the scales out of order, you can. The same thing applies to rituals and magic. Once you learn the basics and fundamentals, then you can put them in whatever order you wish. Keep this in mind over the course of this chapter. What I'm providing you are things I have learned and utilized. Try them. If you don't like them or they don't fit, then you can make the necessary adjustments, but you will at least have them in your wheelhouse. Once you learn the rules of magic, then you can break them. Having a personal spiritual path does not mean doing whatever you want and arguing that it is spiritual.

GODS OR NO GODS

Generally speaking, most, but not all, Pagans are polytheistic. This means that they believe in more than one god. Some view the gods and goddesses as unique individuals, separate from one another. Others see all gods as part of a universal whole, as one deity. And yet, a person may see a bit of both. Just as all humans are part of the whole of humanity, but we each have our own personalities. It is okay, and encouraged, to challenge what your perception of God, the nature of the Divine. Your perception of the gods will change and grow as you do.

Being Called

The gods, ancestors, and other entities will often call on people to be in their service to them. The extant can be to a small or large degree. Some will feel this pull so intensely they could not ignore it if they tried with all their might (and some will try). Others will remain unsure if they are being called or not. And still others will never know they are being called or will hear the call but ignore it. It is always your choice if you dedicate your life to service of the gods or if you do what they ask of you. Personally, I have found that being dedicated to the gods comes with vast rewards. Though it is not always easy, I have never regretted my decision.

Have you ever found yourself so attracted to Poseidon (for example) that you find yourself reading and watching everything you can about him? Do you go out and buy Poseidon statues and get Poseidon tattoos? He's calling to you and likely wants to be your patron deity, the main one you work with. What he wants beyond that, well you'll have to ask him about that. When the gods and goddesses call to you, it is not always so obvious. You may be asked to perform one single task for them. If you are paying attention, you'll see the signs. Remember that coincidence doesn't exist in magic, but synchronicity does. Also keep in mind that not everything is a sign. Ask yourself, is there a reason behind this? If you feed the birds in your yard and you wake up and see birds, then this is only a sign that they appreciate the food and not necessarily a calling from the gods.

Starter Gods

There will be some of you who don't feel drawn to a specific god or goddess yet. Or maybe you do but you are not ready to work with them primarily. While you are learning, do not fear branching out and working with deities from a variety of different pantheons. Curiosity is encouraged.

One important thing to remember, never command a god. The spells provided in this book *invite* a god or goddess to join you. While you can command an element (earth, air, fire, water) to be present, you will be met with much unpleasantness if you attempt to command the gods.

I'm giving you a list of some gods and goddesses that are either easily approachable, are easy to research, or that have an affinity for the previously incarcerated. They are not necessarily "gods for neophytes (newbies)," because some experienced practitioners work with the deities on this list. But they do tend to be easier for inexperienced Pagans to work with.

> *Thoth:* First on the list is the Egyptian god Thoth. What I like about working with Thoth is that he is a real master of wisdom in a variety of subjects. He knows about science, math, writing, and magic, and he is also a messenger. His versatility gives him appeal for many different people. On a side note, there is a well-known tarot deck named after him.

> *Ma'at:* This Egyptian goddess is known to represent order and bring forward truth. She embodies justice. You can call on her to bring order into a chaotic life. Whenever you work with a god or goddess of justice, make sure you stay on the right side of it. They don't play favorites.

> Note to PO:
>
> Ma'at is a good goddess to have in your office. She helps ensure order and that all interactions occurring are just and fair.

> *Hermes/Mercury:* This Greek god, and his Roman counterpart, are the messengers of the gods. If you struggle with hearing messages or feeling like your words are being heard, then call on Hermes or Mercury to help you express yourself.

> *Gaia/Minerva:* Mother Earth in the Greek pantheon is Gaia; her Roman equivalent is Minerva. They

are great goddesses to start with because they have a maternal energy, able to be compassionate but also call forth a tornado if she needs to.

Danu: When I was in prison, Danu was my patron. She came to me and helped me feel like someone was watching over me. This Celtic goddess is a mother goddess but also has strong associations to poetry, wisdom, and art.

Ogma: Another Celtic deity, he is the god of language and learning. He is credited with the creation of ogham, a system of writing used in Wales, Ireland, and the British Isles from the fourth to tenth century CE. If you want to learn ogham, there are few deities as equipped to help you ask Ogma.

Thor: Perhaps one of the best-known Norse gods even in his own time, Thor has seen a resurgence in popularity lately. This red-headed god is the protector of humanity. His hammer, Mjölnir, is a symbol of strength worn by many modern Pagans. Thor is also known for his strength and healing capability.

Freyja: Also spelled Freya, this Norse goddess is more than she first appears. A lot of people think of her as a goddess of love, but more than that, she is also goddess of war. This speaks to her versatility and her ability to know when to give a helping hand and when to wield a sword. So, if you find yourself in two very different life roles, call on Freyja to help you finesse between the two.

The Morrigan: This Celtic goddess calls on many who are, or have been, incarcerated. Her propensity to be drawn to the darkness makes her a good patron for any who are working on their shadow self. People who are on parole tend to be aware of their shadow self, so the connection makes sense.

Cernunnos: Cernunnos, the Celtic "Horned God," oversees all things in nature. He is the stag and the fecundity of the earth. He is part of the primal male archetype, nurturing, virile, consort, who also lets his spirit run free. Regardless of your gender, Cernunnos can help you access that part of yourself that desires to know what it truly means to be free.

Communing with Deity

Communing with deity can be a big part of walking the path. Now, deity can mean whatever shape the Divine takes for you, be it goddess, god, universe, energy, Gaia, Pan, Ymir, whatever you are comfortable with. Part of the appeal of the Pagan faiths is that we don't need an intermediary to have a conversation with the Divine. If you hold the view that God is everything and you are part of everything then you must, by definition, contain the Divine. How beautiful is that? This is why I don't believe in the perfection of the gods. A quick review of myths from nearly any pantheon will show you that they can be quite human at times, especially when it comes to lust, jealousy, and a quest for frivolity.

What this means for communication is that we can have a conversation with them and find things to talk about and bond over. Do you like to ski? Know who else does, the Norse giantess Skaði. There are nine Greek muses you can get to know. Talk to Terpsichore if you are a fan of dance, Euterpe if you are a fan of music, and Clio if you love history. And the Celtic Cernunnos loves to hunt. You don't just have to call on the gods, ancestors, and other beings when you need something. It is okay to just talk to them.

Patron Deity

There is nothing that says that you must have a patron deity, deity you mainly work with. And, even if you have a patron deity, you are not limited to working with only that deity. Many people will have a patron goddess and a patron god. Usually, you'll know who your patron god/dess is because you are either very drawn to them, or you find yourself working with them a lot. Over the course of a lifetime, your patron deity may change. They may change more than once. This is because as you change and learn life lessons, the type of guidance and strength you need will also change. You can simply thank your former patron for all they have given you and move on, or you can put together a ritual to honor the transition.

Prayer

Some of you just tensed up at the sight of this word, I can feel it. But that's okay. A lot of people who are Pagan had upbringings that left them with a strong distaste for anything even mildly religious. Fear not, prayer does not belong to any one group or religion. It is simply a term to describe having a conversation with deity. When Pagans do rituals and spells, this is a type of prayer. The last section covered talking to deity, this is also a type of prayer. Try to get the image of kneeling by your bedside begging for good graces out of your mind. We do sometimes kneel at the altar, but when we do it is out of reverence, not supplication.

Offerings

Just this morning, I put the offerings from my altar outside. As I sprinkled and cast the various nuts and seeds into the yard, a large gust of wind came in. I could feel the gods and the ancestors thanking me for the offering. It does not always get this reaction, but when it does, it is very reaffirming that they appreciate the work I do on their behalf. Offerings do not have to be big and elaborate, though they can be. It is good practice to periodically burn a candle or bake some cookies as an offering for all the gods have granted. Just asking for stuff gets old, for both parties. Frequent gratitude feels good.

Meditation

Meditation is covered in other places throughout this book. I mention it here only to reiterate that it is a way to connect to the Divine.

Spend Time in Nature

If you live in the city, the noise, both audible and energetic, can make it hard to connect to the natural world. Make it a point to do something in nature on a regular basis. This can include camping, going for a hike, sitting by a river, gardening, or even just taking off your shoes and walking in the grass.

Learn Mythology

The folklore that exists from the pre- and post-Christian eras is vast. I'm not suggesting that you try to learn every story from every culture that has ever existed. What I am suggesting is that if you are working with a particular goddess or god, especially more than once, that you read some of their legends. This helps you to understand them and what they may like and not like.

MAGIC BASICS

Many think of magic as being supernatural, something outside of self. Really though, it is quite natural. We are born with it. Think about children "playing" fairies, stirring mud potions, or having a fascination with dragons. It is because they are born knowing the magical world intuitively and instinctively. They remember. No one must teach a child how to play. They know.

Oomph Scale

There are many spells that have been provided to you throughout this book. Some of you may be asking, how do I know if it was successful? Well, if you have a clear, short-term goal (getting a job for example) then you'll know it worked because you'll get a job. Others don't have such a definitive outcome, so how do you know if it worked. Well, spells always work, just not always to the degree you wish. Imagine you are trying to fill a bucket with water. You add one drop, and the bucket is not full, but you are closer to your goal. So, it worked. You are now closer to your goal, but you are not done yet. Magic can be like this, especially when you are a neophyte (newbie or seeker).

There are a couple of different approaches you can take regarding the strength of your spell. Think about a scale, one of those old fashion kinds with the arms and the two plates. Now imagine that one side is weighed down. There are a few ways you can tip the scales in your favor. One is that you can gather a bunch of little stones and stack them until you have enough weight. Another is that you can gather a few medium stones. Or last you can get one big stone and use that to tip the scales. In magic, the size of the stone you are using depends on the quality of your spell, I call this magical oomph. And magical oomph, in conjunction with how much energy it takes to achieve the goal of your spell, will determine how successful your spell will be.

Magical Correspondences

When it comes time to craft (pun intended) a spell or ritual, there are countless correspondences you can use to help you focus your energy. You can get stones, herbs, candle colors, chants, and scents to all match your intention. For many of you, you will feel these things instinctively. For others, you will need a reference book for a while. A little tip, you do not need 45 different books of correspondence and you do not need to memorize, nor hand copy, all the correspondences. There are better ways to utilize your time. One good correspondence book can serve you well. Provided it is your book and not one on loan, you can always add to it and expand it by writing in the margins or using sticky notes.

Using correspondences adds oomph to you working. Let's say you are doing a spell for money. Having a green candle anointed with mint oil, coins on the altar, and money symbols from various cultures can help the universe, the gods, home in on what you are asking for. Visualization is still important, but these corresponding items and colors help you tune into the vibration of what you are seeking, in this case money.

Ways to Ensure Successful Magic

Many neophytes start off with the small pebbles, there's nothing wrong with that but eventually you want more bang for your buck. Also, avoid the urge to think that this means you will need to do every spell dozens of times to be successful. *You are more powerful than you know.* Thinking about how close you are to completing your goal can help you to put it in perspective. If you have already put applications in for jobs, then the magic for the job spell doesn't have to achieve as much, fewer strings need to be pulled. There are many things you can do that will help ensure your spells success. We'll talk about these next.

Focus

Avoid distraction when doing magical work. Be completely present in the moment. If you are thinking about what to make for dinner or what time you must pick up your kids or anything else mundane, then you are deflating your magical intention. When you focus you are sending a clear image to the gods of what you are asking for. If there is a stray thought of mac and cheese, then the request gets confused. The more of these side messages you have, the more distorted the message becomes. Remember the strength of your magic depends on your level of your focus. Meditation helps you to develop this skill. But you should also do things like, leave your cell phone on silent and in another room, eat something nutritious beforehand, take deep breaths, and don't try to fit a spell in a short period of time.

Patience

Things will not always happen in your time frame; they will happen in the time frame of the universe. And, since time is a man-made concept anyway, you will do well to have a bit of patience when awaiting outcomes. Something you can do, if you need results sooner rather than later is to add "without hassle or delay" to your spells. The universe doesn't understand Tuesday at 5 p.m. but does understand that sometimes you need rush delivery. Sometimes a delay can have long-term benefits. Do not assume that because you didn't instantly manifest what you were looking for that it means your spell didn't work. Time … takes time.

Trust

Trusting yourself and your spell work will not come naturally to some of you, it didn't for me at first. There were so many things I had messed up in my life I barely trusted myself to pick out toothpaste on my own. If you find yourself in the same boat, it's normal. It's okay. And you can learn to trust yourself. Start with small things, whatever that looks like to you. If you've never picked out your own shoes go pick out a pair. There are only a few possible outcomes, you'll like them, or you won't. If you don't then you don't have to buy those anymore. It is not the end of the world. You can resell them or give them away. In order to learn to trust yourself you need to let yourself make mistakes AND learn from those mistakes. It might help you to make a pro/con list or to write out all possible consequences of each choice.

Once you can trust yourself, at least a little, to do mundane things, then you can learn to trust yourself to do magical things. Remember, we are all born knowing how to tap into the magic of the universe. If you do a spell "wrong," the world is not going to explode. It will be just like buying those shoes. If it goes well, keep doing what you're doing. If it doesn't you know what not to do next time. Trust that whatever you do in the magical world will either be a success, be a lesson, or both.

Priest/Priestess Voice

Your casting voice is your voice, but the strongest version of it. Not meek or timid, but in command, a master of the universe. It is not your voice when you are shouting or screaming but it is still heard. You will know when you've hit it because it will have a resonance to it that is uniquely yours. Imagine your kids or a friend's kid is about to climb over a railing at the zoo into the lion area. You are too far away to grab them, so you look them in the eye and say NO with command. They know you mean business. This is so close to what your casting voice should be that you can start here and fine tune it. The difference is that your casting voice doesn't contain that element of fear. In fact, it contains no emotions, just focus, self-confidence, and assuredness. Practice this voice and see the difference it makes in your spell work.

Not Talking About Spells

When you do a spell, it is like you are filling a balloon with air and sending it to the desired location. When you talk about you spells with others you are inviting people to throw darts at and deflate your balloon, especially if you include details. All it takes is someone saying "that won't work" to throw doubt into the mix and have you questioning your magic. Even well-meaning friends may think such thoughts when you tell them, adding an energy of doubt. There are a couple of exceptions I have found. The first is if you are gaining advice about how to do a spell *before* you do it. The second is if you are working your magic with another person or in a group. There may still be doubt, but when you have many people focusing on one goal, it also adds oomph. The third is if the spell has already run its course and it is being used as an example to teach another with.

Nothing Comes from Nothing

In an earlier chapter, I talked about scientific principles and how they relate to magic. You might recall that energy can neither be created not destroyed, only transformed. This means that you can't manifest something from nothing. However, it doesn't have to be something physical that you use to create this energy exchange. When you put physical effort behind something, like putting in applications to supplement a job spell, you are transforming action into outcome. There are other ways to do this as well. Devoting time to philanthropic endeavors, dancing to raise energy in circle, singing to raise energy, spending all day baking cookies to offer the Goddess, tending a garden, all of these require time and energy that can be put towards your goal. Set your intention beforehand and your effort will go where it is needed.

One thing to remember: when doing any magical work, energy for spells should not come from you. Your energy is limited. The energy of the universe and the earth is infinite. Proper grounding and centering, before and after, allow you to tap into this infinite energy source. If you find yourself drained after ritual, you did not ground properly and were using your own energy supply.

Visualization

Close your eyes. Now, visualize the room you are in. How detailed is the image in your closed eyes? Now open your eyes, study a part of the room for a moment, then try again. Did the image improve? Hopefully, it did. When you want to manifest something from the universe, you want to see it as clearly in your mind as you can. If you want help getting a house, then see it, the trim, the colors, where the stairs are. What do you see when the front door is open? The more real it is to you, the more the universe is called to manifest it.

Some people have a hard time "seeing" in their mind's eye. You can try this exercise with smell, sound, and touch if these are stronger senses for you. The point is to make your intent as real as possible. If you can smell the smell of your new car, then do that. And yes, you absolutely can use all your senses to "visualize" it.

MAGICAL TERMS AND PRACTICES

Now, let's get into some of the traditional accepted terms and practices that are used magically. The following descriptions aren't about doing things right or wrong. Most of you reading this book are new to the craft and to the Pagan faith. You must start somewhere. These are good places to start.

Deasil vs. Widdershins

These are jargon for clockwise (deasil) and counterclockwise (widdershins). It is traditional that if you want something to increase you move in a deasil manner. If you want to decrease something, you move widdershins. For those that cast circle, you move around it deasil to start the circle and widdershins to take it down at the end. These directions can be used in a lot of ways. If you want to imbue your soup with positive energy, stir deasil. If you want your soup to help banish negative thoughts, stir widdershins, each time focusing on your desired outcome as you do so.

Phases of the Moon

The moon has a direct impact on the ebb and flow of the tides, the pull of the water in our bodies, and can help "pull" your magic in on direction or another. The cycle of the moon goes new moon, when the moon is not visible in the sky to full moon, when she is a big glowing orb. The time from new moon to full moon is called a waxing moon, the moon will get bigger. From the full moon to the new moon, when the moon is getting smaller, is called waning. If you want something to increase, use the energy of the waxing moon. If you want something to decrease, use the energy of the waning moon. What if you really need to do a spell and the moon is the wrong phase? You do it anyway. Use other correspondences (day, time of day, colors, etc. ...) if available to add magical oomph.

Using the Element

Earth, air, fire, water, and spirit (the culmination of all five) are the traditional elements used in magical practices. Each element has an associated direction and color. Though these vary in some tradition, typically you will find that earth is associated with the north and given either green or brown as a correspondence. Air will have east and yellow. Fire will be south and red. Then water, will be west and blue. While you are starting off, have a representation of each element on your altar.

Invoke vs. Evoke

Many people use these terms interchangeably, but they have two separate meanings. When you evoke a deity or spirit you are asking it to join you in your sacred space. When you invoke, you are taking that energy into yourself. Evoking deity means they are in your presence, invoking deity means they are within you. Invoking is extremely challenging and should not be taken on by anyone who is not adept. Evoking deity, though, that is something you can start doing early on.

Burying

Burying items is an old magic. It is a way of giving them to the earth to be transformed and remade. This being said, make sure that the items you are burying are natural and not harmful to the environment. Seeds, stones, natural parchment, and other items work well depending on their intended purpose. If your intent involves wanting to keep something around, bury it in your back yard. If you want it to go away, bury it in your front yard.

Never evoke what you can't banish: There are different levels and skill sets in magic. This isn't hierarchical making one spell better than another. But there are undoubtedly some things that takes more skill than others. Generally speaking, if you are meditating, chanting, calling on various entities, and the like, you're fine and completely safe. But I'll give you an example of a situation you will want to be careful in. Most people think of fairies as these cute, delicate, and whimsical little beings. While they think they are hilarious, they are tricksters and can be quite troublesome. If you don't believe me, read about changelings and bean sidhe (banshee) sometime. They also come in many forms with many different personalities. If you call on fairies and they start taking off with things or causing trouble, what are you going to do about it? So, do your research first. If you move into deeper trancework, spell work, invocations, high seat rituals, working with unfamiliar energetic beings, and that kind of thing, do your homework first and make sure that you have a good foundation in the basics. Don't assume everything is harmless.

WRITING RITUALS

One of the most fun and creative aspects of magic is getting to write your own spells and rituals, then do them. These have a bit of extra oomph because you put the energy into writing them. You can make them as individual as you are. If you like are artistic or musical, add this as a piece of the ritual. If you have welding skills, then make a metal statue or offering as part of the rite. As you read through each section, ask yourself "how can I make this uniquely mine?"

Intent: The first thing you will want to know is what is the purpose of the rite or spell. If you are creating a spell for prosperity, it is going to have a different feel than a Samhain ritual. Once you decide what your intent it, you can develop and hone it from there.

Correspondence

Next, pick out corresponding colors, scents, days of the week, astrological phases, herbs, stones, and deities that match your intention. When referencing your correspondences, look beyond just the intention. For example, with a money spell, mint is a corresponding herb. Anything that corresponds with mint will also correspond with money.

Meditation

Yes, you can write your own meditation if you feel up to the task. Or you can use a prepared meditation that suits your purpose and matches your intent. The meditation you pick doesn't have to be super serious either. Sometimes, it is fun to go swim under ocean waves without a specific goal. I'm also fond of free form meditations where I just let myself be taken to places.

To Rhyme or Not to Rhyme

In Wicca, there tends to be a propensity for spells that rhyme. And rhyming spells do certainly have a lovely flow and cadence to them. But, there is something to be said for standing before the gods and letting the words from your heart flow out of your mouth and into the air around you. Early on, it is a good idea to write you evocations and chants beforehand so that the energy of your ritual doesn't get disturbed. Try to memorize sections. If this isn't possible, at least read through the words out loud before the ritual to assess how they feel.

Listen to Instinct

Just because you didn't write random clapping into your ritual doesn't mean you shouldn't do it when it feels right. There will be times when you are performing a spell or participating in ritual, and you will feel this urge to do something that hadn't occurred to you before. Don't ignore this. You are in the space between world during these times. This means that deity and spirits and ancestral beings can inspire and communicate with you, even if you are not consciously aware of it. The conscious mind speaks the language of facts and functionality. It, too, often blocks out the subconscious mind which knows dreams and stories and all things that can't be quantified. If you are getting urges to celebrate in ritual, these are coming from or through your subconscious ... let it speak.

Be Creative

Every single one of you has strengths and skills. Do not be afraid to use these in your ritual design. If you know herbs, then by all means get out your mortar and pestle and blend some herbs to burn for the occasion. Are you crafty by nature, then create something that expresses your intent? And yes, if you cook and that is your thing, then put together a meal or beverage which contains corresponding ingredients to suit your purpose. The idea, ultimately, is not to read a spell out of book and have that be the end. Sure, you may start off like that. But rituals are expressive and adaptive and alive in a way. Any spell or rite that appears in any book I write, you may change to make yours. I seek only to provide a starting point on which you may build.

WALKING THE PATH

What does it mean to walk a Pagan path? Well for me, it means a lot of things. On one hand it means living my life in a way that if I am the only Pagan a person ever meets, they would be willing to meet another. It also means that I stand up for what I believe in and yet remain willing to change my mind when new evidence is presented. It means practicing self-care and still caring for others. It means that I will be a little different, hopefully better, version of myself than I was yesterday. The more important question here is what does walking the path mean to you? Really think about it. Nature is a sacred force, you are part of nature, so you are also sacred. Do you treat yourself as if you are sacred? Shouldn't you start? Let's take a moment and look at some of the things that might make up the essence of your path. While these are simply suggestions, they are suggestions that have been tested by many people and found to be successful,

- Taking ownership of what's yours
- Not taking ownership for what's not
- Take the high road
- Pay attention
- Meditate regularly
- Practice random acts of kindness (without expecting a reward)
- Welcome challenges

SEALING SPELL

This spell is to seal away a behavior or thought which no longer serves you. Let me clarify that this spell does not mean you will never experience that thought or find yourself about to act on a behavior. What it does is helps you to become aware of it so that you can make the choice to act on it or do something about it. The ability to seal something away is a good basic tool for your magical arsenal. The outline provided here can be adapted to help you seal away people, places, and things, that no longer benefit you.

What You Need

- A dark blue candle
- Paper (parchment if available)
- A wax seal (a metal butter knife will also work)
- Sealing wax
- Pen or quill and ink
- A fireproof container to burn your petition
- Cakes and juice—any natural cookie, cake, juice, or tea will work.

Spell

If you choose to, cast circle. If not, move on to the next step.

> Earth mother Gaia, in whose womb all creation begins and ends
> Join me now to help my flaws to mend.

Light the candle.

Close your eyes and breathe deeply three times.

See the behavior you are trying to get rid of appearing between your hands. It may appear as a word or an image. However it appears, see it clearly.

Write the word on the paper. See it shifting from hands to pen to paper.

When you have written the word and can "see" the image on the paper, then begin to fold in the corners of the paper so the meet in the middle. The words should be inside the folds. Fold the corners again towards the same side.

Take your sealing wax and warm it over the candle until it begins to melt. Drip some into the middle of the paper where all the corners meet. Then, use your wax sealer to press it down.

Hold the paper over the candle until it catches and say,

> I seal you (behavior)
> And cast you away far from me,
> I need you no longer,
> With this act, I set me free.
> I burn you first within my hearth
> I give you now to Mother Earth.

Put the paper in the fireproof container and let it burn down to ash.

If you cast circle, now is the time to open it.

After the ashes have cooled bury them in the earth so that Gaia can transform them into something else. Leave her the food and pour the drink out onto the earth as offerings to her. Say "I offer this with thanks."

DEDICATION RITUAL

A dedication ritual is intended to provide you with a ritual that will signify to you, and the gods, that you are ready to undergo a period dedicated to living life as a Pagan. Most people will perform their dedication and renew it after a year-and-a-day. If, after this time, you decide that Paganism isn't for you, you are free to move on to something else. No ire, no ill will from the gods or spirits, simply a mutual understanding that you tried it and it wasn't.

You will need time to complete this ritual and a space where you will not be interrupted. You may want to take a camping trip or find an outdoor space to have this ritual in. Beforehand, you will want to find the deity you would like to work with primarily for the next 366 days. The ones with connection to education are good choices, but not your only choices. For this ritual, I am using the Norse goddess Saga.

Preparation

Write down some words you want to say to the deity of your choice. Are you asking for guidance over this next year? Support? Wisdom? Growth? Put down a few sentences stating what you would like their role to be.

If you are camping in a place that allows it, build a bonfire. Be sure to have water to put the fire out when you are done.

What You Need

- A representation of each element, for example:
  › Fire: Candle or the bonfire
  › Water: A cup of water or access to a lake or river
  › Earth: A bowl of earth
  › Air: A feather of incense. The smoke from the fire also works.
- Food and drink for offering.
- Candle to represent deity.
- Matches.
- A piece of ritual jewelry. It doesn't have to be expensive, but something you are comfortable wearing.
- Words you've prepared.

Ritual

Set up the items around you, light the bonfire, and breathe deeply. Spend a few moments thinking about why you are here. What is the purpose of this ritual? What does it mean to you? What do you hope to gain? What do you hope to give? If you have any fears or doubts, now is the time to give them to the universe. You will be fine. The space you are in is one that is safe, secure, and where you are one with all nature.

Stand in front of the bonfire, arms outstretched and say,

> Here in this hour, I seek guidance from an ancient power. I stand to seek, learn, and gain all I need for the next year-and-day.

Light your candle for Saga. Then say:

> Goddess, I invite you here on this night, I ask you to attend this dedication and to witness this rite. Hail and welcome, Saga!

Now, you will use the elements one at a time to fulfil a specific part of your initiation.

You'll start with fire. Place your hands and body just close enough to the bonfire to feel it's warmth. You should avoid standing so close that it will burn you.

As you stand in front of the fire say,

> With the power of fire, I burn away any negative feelings about religions and faiths that I have experienced before. I do this so that fresh seeds may be laid.

Rinse your hands and face with the water and say,

With this water, I wash away all my preconceived ideas about Paganism. I open myself up to feeling each experience as it comes.

Take a handful of earth and hold it in your hands, smell its scent and say,

With the power of earth, I allow my body, mind, and spirit to be nourished for growth. I take each step with trust that my path is always before me.

Take in a deep breath while holding the feather in your hand and say:

With the power of air, my mind is open to wisdom I may receive. Each breath I take connects me to the gods.

In your priest/ess voice say words you've prepared to deity. Then throw them into the fire and let them be carried up into the sky.

Take the piece of jewelry you have acquired and run it by each element saying,

As each element clears, creates, stabilizes, and unites so they pass these qualities onto you, my sacred symbol that I am ready to take this next step on my journey.

Put the jewelry on and say,

Let this _____ represent my vow to study Paganism, in any or all its forms for the next year and a day. After which, I may renew my vow or go a separate way. Huzzah.

Take some of your offering drink and hold it up to the sky. Say:

For Saga and any who have joined me in this rite.

Pour some out for her, then take a drink.

With my thanks.

Take some of your offering food and hold it up to the sky. Say,

For Saga and any who have joined me in this rite.

Place some on the ground for her, then take a drink.

With my thanks.

If you leave Saga's candle burning, make sure you stay awake until it has burned out. It is also appropriate to move the candle to the fire pit and let it burn down there.

Eat and drink in front of the bonfire until you feel ready to take your leave.

The last thing to do is to make sure that your fire is out and all trash that you have brought in is taken with you when you leave. Over the course of the next year-and-a-day, you will be given opportunities to learn and explore many things. What this looks like will be different for each of you. Keep an open mind and trust your instincts. Remember, the gods are with you.

CHAPTER 8
MAGICAL PROTECTION

We all have the right to protect ourselves and our families. We do. This section is going to explore protection. Human beings, we tend to want protection to mean keeping us free from all pain and discomfort. This is understandable, but not necessarily how protection works. Remember from earlier lessons that discomfort is necessary, particularly for the change process. If you lived in a fully protective bubble, you would never really experience life. I mention this so that you don't have unrealistic expectations. If you ride your bike and fall and break a bone, this does mean you were not protected. It means that the accident could have been much worse if you weren't protected.

Like most other things in magic, protection involves us doing our part too. When you work in the realm of protection magic, do not be surprised if lessons come up which teach you how to be cautious or which challenge you to take better care of yourself. Pay attention to the world around you and in time you will learn to see the world in a new way. In an earlier chapter I stated that I have never met anyone who was all light or all darkness. This does not mean however that everyone and everything is harmless. Sometimes it is intentional and sometimes it is not. Either way, knowing how to protect yourself energetically and magically is what this chapter is all about.

MUNDANE ACTIONS

Let's start with the mundane actions. I know, I know, this is a book of magic. But there is a great deal of magic to be found in the mundane, if one knows where to look. First, no amount of protection magic will keep you safe if you intentionally put yourself in harmful situations. You must use some common sense. I don't care how many protective symbols you are carrying, if you poke a lion in the face, they will probably attack you.

I'm not going to go into a lot of detail about mundane actions because you know what they are. Things like locking your doors at night, wearing your seatbelt, and not walking down sketchy alleyways should be obvious. Other things like mental and physical health are discussed in more detail in other chapters of this book.

BOUNDARIES

Boundary setting is a skill. Like any skill it takes practice to get good at it. Even if you are good at it, this is a valuable skill worth perfecting because it is essential to having a healthy life. The steps listed should give you a good starting point for developing boundary setting skills. They only work if you put them into action when it matters though. This is discussed in more detail in other chapters, but here's the quick list.

- *Start small:* Set a small boundary with a trusted friend and go from there.
- *Get support and advice:* If it is a challenge for you, get help. Ask counselors or spiritual advisors for tips if you need to.

- *Be clear and direct with your words:* Don't use qualifiers such as "sometimes" and "maybe." These leave your message open to interpretation.

- *Be steadfast:* Being flexible is a good thing, but if you have said no to something you really don't want to do, stand by your no.

- *No is a complete sentence:* You don't need to explain, justify, or quantify your no.

- *Give yourself permission:* You don't need to have something else planned to say no. If you don't want to do something, that is reason enough.

- *Listen to your body:* How many people behind bars have a story that starts off like "I knew I shouldn't have …" or "I just felt it in my bones." This is your intuition speaking to you.

- *Self-care after the boundary is set:* If you find yourself shaking after confrontation know that it goes away in time. For now, breathe deeply and know that you did good.

- *Visualize your boundary:* It can help to imagine yourself drawing a line in the sand and stating what cannot cross it.

WHEN SHOULD I ENERGETICALLY PROTECT MYSELF?

We're going to get real for a moment. In my last book, *Paganism for Prisoners: Connecting to the Magic Within*, I discuss how everything is energy. You are energy. The sun is energy. Dogs, cats, trees, thoughts, tables, all energy. Because we are energy, it is common to pick up on the energy of others and have their energy affect yours. Some people who are more sensitive to this energy exchange are called empaths. If you find your mood and/ or thoughts easily swayed based on the people you hang around, then protecting yourself energetically will make a difference and prevent you from picking up what is not yours.

There are many reasons to protects yourself energetically. I want you to think back to a time when you were in a crowd of people. How did you feel? Were you excited? Anxious? Overwhelmed? Super charged? How about after? In groups, though not just large ones, the energetic vibrations can have an impact on how you feel and how you present to the world. To stay in your center, it is good to energetically protect yourself anytime you are headed into a situation where you may find yourself anxious, overwhelmed, or uncomfortable. Or, if being around a large group really revs you up and causes you to go out of your way to be the center of focus, even to the extent of doing dangerous or ill-advised things, then you should also energetically protect yourself. The goal being to stay your most true self and not be swayed by the energies of others.

There are other external reasons to protect your energy field, such as to prevent psychic attacks, decrease electronic interference, and to reduce contact from astral beings such as ghosts, spirits, and other entities. But there are many internal reasons to protect yourself. First, if you can receive energy from others, you can send it to others. Some people have such a strong energy field that their emotions can alter the feel of an entire room. Second, if you don't have a particularly strong or cohesive energy field, you may inadvertently cling onto and pull from the energy field of another. You may even find yourself dependent on them instead of independent within yourself. Third, it will keep you balanced, more able to handle the ups and downs of life.

Note to PO:

Shielding, and the other energy protections methods mentioned, can be of a great benefit to you as well. You deal with many people from day-to-day and week-to-week. There will be many parolees you will have that are particularly sensitive to energies. If they come into your office and pick up on the negativity from the person before them, this will seep in like a disease. By shielding, you can protect them and yourself. It is likely to even make your day go better.

Psychic Attacks

Though it is not common, there are some people who do not have a suitable energetic resonance for their body system to sustain itself in a state of homeostasis. They may inadvertently "feed" off the energy of others to enhance their own body system. Psychic vampire is a common term used to describe these people; however, it has some connotations that are not accurate, and I think people tend to use the term as an umbrella for people who are abusive, snarky, manipulative, etc. Or it gets used as a reason for people not to work on themselves or attend to their wellness... "I don't need to see a doctor; it is obviously so-and-so attacking me."

Intentional psychic attacks are also rare. It takes a lot of focus and energetic control to influence the thoughts and emotions of others without their willingness. By the time one develops skills such as these, they usually lose the desire to misuse or abuse them. It is much like martial arts where you develop the discipline to know when not to use your skills, not just the ability to use them. This being said, there are symptoms that, when presenting without a known cause, may indicate that someone is attaching to your energy field or pulling through it. If you experience these, it is a good idea to shield yourself and see if this improves your symptoms.

> *Insomnia:* In this case, it is insomnia which is prolonged and without any sort of physical explanation. It is normal to have the occasional sleepless night. This is even more true if you have just gone through something traumatic, moved to a new time zone, started new medication, are ill, or if you have sudden diet changes. But if you can rule physical causes and the usual sleep methods aren't working, it is possible someone is psychically attacking you.

> *Constant bad dreams:* This is a sign to watch out for particularly if you are suddenly having bad dreams, having bad dreams that are more vivid, or of a particular person always makes an appearance. Symbolism is significant too particularly if the dreams involve horrific accidents, loss of limb, loss of life, or if you have trouble waking up from them. Rule out diet, time zone changes, changes to your sleep schedule, and a guilty conscience as possible causes.

> *Excessive illness, malaise, or lack of energy:* There have been many recent scientific studies on the causes of weak vs. strong immune systems. For example, children who are exposed to day-to-day germs in their youth tend to grow into adults with stronger immune systems, they built natural immunity. This is important because I don't

want any of you thinking that if you have a child that gets sick a lot that they are necessarily under a hex or being psychically attacked. What this does refer to is sudden illness without a cause, fine one day, seriously ill the next. Or if you are normally energetic then find yourself without energy for months. See the difference? Only you know what your "normal" is. Maybe you are usually low energy, but it is worse than it has ever been. The key here is not to compare yourself to others, but to look for illness, malaise, and lack of energy that vary from your norm.

Hearing, sensing, seeing dark entities: Out of all the symptoms and signs on this list, this can be one of the most unnerving. Some people are gifted with clairaudience, clairvoyance, or other clair-senses that will make them more vulnerable to seeing, hearing, and sensing entities. You will want to listen to your instinct and your gut to determine if the intent of the entities and energies you are seeing.

Among the other signs that you may be under psychic attack are breaking glass or lights exploding (without cause), consistent sense of uneasiness or like you are being watched, excessive bad luck, and unusual physical pain that doesn't have a diagnosable cause. When you are confronted with these symptoms, perform the cleansing located at the end of this chapter and use some of the personal protection methods listed in the next section.

PERSONAL PROTECTION

Just as it sounds, personal protection involves techniques you can use to protect yourself. They are also great to teach kids and other loved ones. If your children are too small or furry or scaly or feathered to use these techniques themselves, then you can create a protective orb around them or make an amulet or charm for them to wear. Then, when they become old enough, they can create their own. As has been done previously in this, and other, chapters we will start with the mundane then move to the magical. This gives us a good segue into the first form of protection, choosing whose company you keep.

Physically Cleanse

If you are going somewhere, you can do a quick and effective protection by putting some sea salt in a damp washcloth and rubbing in all over your body. This is a great witchy tip to keep handy if you find yourself called to some last-minute engagement and want some protection. As you wipe the washcloth all over you, know that it is forming a protective barrier. All magic starts in our thoughts. When you get home, repeat the process on areas that feel "mucky" or "muddled."

Shielding

Shielding is a powerful way to protect your energy field. I make it a habit to shield myself anytime I will be at an event with people I don't know, when I feel not strongest, when my intuition tells me to, and sometimes just because. The more you practice shielding, the easier it will become, until finally it becomes second nature. There are dozens of ways you can shield; I'll give you some of my favorites to get you started.

They mostly begin the same way. You will take a few deep breaths and bring your awareness into yourself. Then focus on your feet and where the touch the ground. Visualize the energy from the earth coming up in through your feet and into your body. Bring up energy from the earth until it fills your body. When you feel full of earth energy, pick one of the following methods to create your shield. You will be directing this earth energy out to surround your body.

Shields

Have you ever seen one of those TV shows where a group of soldiers surround themselves with shields? Well, this is the basic idea. All the energy you just got from the earth, form it into shields that protects all sides of you. Some people use an orb of energy and have it surround them on all sides. The fun thing about this method is that you can use any color, style, or shape of shield you like. Mine are usually large and wooden and painted with dragons. But play around with them. Just make sure there are enough to completely surround you.

Mirror Ball

Think of the image of a disco ball or mirror ball. All those little mirrors reflecting outward. They create a perfect reflective surface that not only keeps you from being impacted by negativity but reflects what is being sent to you back to the sender. More than just reflecting, it changes what bounces off it into beautiful light. To create this, imagine the mirror ball creating a protective orb all around your body. Make sure it goes over your head and under your feet.

Webs/Nets

The spider is a powerful animal, and sadly misunderstood. When you use a web to surround yourself, you can catch the things you don't want and wrap them up. They become trapped. Then, when you take down the web, they dissipate along with it. Spider energy is quite powerful. This weaver can take what gets caught in her web and use it to give herself strength and vitality. When you think about it like that, protective web energy can do what few other types of protection can; it can help you turn something you don't want in your energy into something that benefits you in the long run. Something important to note is that if you use the web of protection, you should be respectful to the spiders you meet. If you don't want them in your house, catch and release whenever possible. A net can be used if you are an arachnophobe. It is still effective but lacks the transformative spider energy found with a web.

Castle Walls (with or without Fire-Breathing Dragons)

Out of all the shielding techniques I have used, this is one of my favorites. Who doesn't love a nice stone castle with drawbridge and a moat? Just like the others, you will want to envision castle walls surrounding you. If you want knights, dragons, archers, or anything else to increase your protection, well these fit quite well into this protective visualization. To make this really powerful try to sense what the walls feel like? What sounds and smells you can make out? What does the ground beneath you feel like? The more real it is to you, the more effective it will be. This one has the added benefit of a draw bridge if you want to let someone else's energy into your field.

Wall of Thorns

This is very similar in idea to the methods listed previously. This one is fun though because you can visualize (and hear) the thorns growing from the earth below and surrounding you. These thorns can be any color and as long as you want. I recommend that you have the actual thorns pointing out, not in, but they will grow as they are meant to. To take this wall down, they can recede back into the earth, or you can visualize a wicked pair of hedge clippers in your hand and cut your way out.

Omnil

An omnil is a three-dimensional shape that surrounds you. It is different from an orb because it has a specific way it must be cast. Instead of being like an eggshell, it is three moving rings that intersect at 90° angles of one another. Though omnils can be used for many purposes, the one I give you here will be for the purpose of protection. It takes good visualization skills to get this down, so make sure you have practiced this skill before attempting an omnil.

You will want to imagine it as electric blue while you are casting it. Each of the sections represents time, space, and events respectively. You can use either an athame, a wand, or your hands to cast though the athame does tend to have the longest lasting results. Over time, the omnil will fall apart by itself. The length of time it stays will depend on the focus used to cast it.

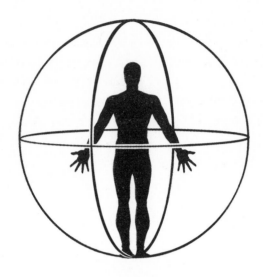

Before you begin, you will want to focus on what you don't want. If you are trying to protect yourself from someone specific, focus on them. If you are trying to protect yourself in general, you can focus on feeling unsafe while you cast. In this way, an omnil is quite different from other magical forms. I see it as working like a magical vaccine where you teach the rings what to be aware of so they can spot it sooner and prevent it.

First, you will cast the horizontal ring that represents time. In a clockwise motion, and horizontally around your body cast the first ring. Start at your front and finish there. Make sure to bring it full circle.

Second is the one that represents space. Starting at the top of your head draw your ring clockwise down to the right of your body, then under your feet and up the left side of your body. Once again, complete the ring at the top.

Third is events. Start at the top of your head and go behind you to the floor, under your feet, up the front of your body, and enclose it at the top.

You are now surrounded by an electric blue shield of protection. If you find that you need to take down your omnil, you either need to use the same tool you used to create it or wait for it to dissipate on its own.

Protective Amulet

An amulet is an item which is worn or hung up to ward off negativity and evil. Yes, it is okay to buy your amulets, just be sure to cleanse them with some salt and water or sage before you use them. The symbols provided here can be used for personal or home protection.

Nazar / Nazar Boncuğu

Better known as the evil eye in the western world, the nazar is a Middle Eastern symbol that protects the wearer from the undo influences of the evil eye. Like when someone is giving you that sideways eye. The nazar can be an amulet or drawn on paper, painted, put on a block of wood, painted on a mirror; it is truly versatile. For maximum effectiveness, have it pointing outward, such as on your window facing the outer world or facing your front door.

Pentagram/Pentacle

These are probably two of the best-known images in Wicca and Paganism. The oldest pentagrams (note they are not surrounded by a circle) have been found on pottery from Ancient Sumer from 3500 BCE. Later, the symbol shows up in ancient Greece. It has represented deities such as Roman Venus, Greek Chronos, and the Sumerian Marduk and Ishtar. It has represented healing, the five points of the human body, the path that the planet Venus travels, initiation, protection, and much more. The pentacle is a modern adaptation of the pentagram. These are great protective symbols because you can draw them, buy them, carve them, and even make them with a few sticks. All have equal potential for protection.

Mjölnir

Better known as Thor's hammer, this symbol has seen a popular resurgence lately. As the name suggests, it is a symbol for the Norse god Thor. The hammer he wielded, in mythology not comic books, was protective but also imperfect. When it was being forged, Loki turned into a gadfly and stung the dwarf Brokkr in the eye. Brokkr paused the bellows causing Mjölnir to be formed with a handle that was shorter than it should have been. I personally find it an interesting piece of mythology that one of the most powerful tools to ever exist was imperfect. Even Odin determined it to be the greatest treasure made. When you wear this symbol know that you don't have to be imperfect to be powerful and strong.

Luis

An ogham symbol, luis represents the Rowan tree, one of my personal favorites. This tree was sacred to many Pagan cultures and has links to the Celtic goddess Brighid, the Greek Hebe, Thor in Norse mythology, and the Welsh goddess Cerridwen. Two attributes which make it quite protective are the pentagram that shows just beneath the stalk and the vibrant red color of the berries. Red has long been associated with protection.[25]

25. Alan Watson Featherstone, et al., "Rowan Tree Mythology and Folklore," Trees for Life, March 5, 2021, https://treesforlife.org.uk/into-the-forest/trees-plants-animals/trees/rowan/rowan-mythology-and-folklore/.

Eye of Horus

Horus is the Egyptian god of protection, health, and the regenerative cycle of the waning and waxing moon. Horus lost his eye in a struggle with the god Seth only to have it heal later. The Eye of Horus (the left eye), also known as the wedjat eye or udjat eye is one of the most well-known symbols to come from the ancient Egyptian period. It is often mistaken for the Eye of Ra which is the right eye. There is an element of guidance and innate wisdom that you invite in when you wear the Eye of Horus.

HOME PROTECTION

When moving into a new home you won't always know its history, the intimate details of lives that have occurred within those walls. Later in this chapter I give you a three-part protection spell. The second part is dedicated to home protection. You can either start with that, then move onto the home protection methods given here. Or use this spell as a stand-alone. It really depends on how much protection you feel like you want in your home.

Draw Protective Symbols

Step 1: Mix one of the following oils with extra virgin olive oil: Castoreum, storax, orris root, lemonwood, sandalwood, or lavender.

Step 2: Use a single horse, camel, or goat hair to stir them together. Do not harm the animal in the process of getting the hair. You can use a cat whisker that the cat has shed (DO NOT cut a whisker) or discarded feather as an alternative.

Step 3: Draw the following symbol with the oil on your front door, back door, and any other doors that lead outside of your home.

In a commanding voice state "This house is protected. So it shall be."

Black Tourmaline

This is probably one of the simplest protection methods. You just get some black tourmaline, available at most metaphysical stores and rock shops, and you stick a piece in every window and next to every doorway. That's it. Easy, right?

Besoms

It wasn't intentional, but somehow, I found myself with about a dozen besoms in my home. They are in every room. It is a time-honored tradition to have at least one besom by your front door with the bristles pointed up. They are protective and also serve as a portend of unexpected events.

Crossing Water

Evil can't follow you if you cross water. This is a long-held belief that persists in many parts of the world. If you find yourself in a situation where you feel like you are being followed, cross a stream, river, lake, even a large puddle will work in a pinch.

Blood Root/Sanguinaria canadensis

You can either dry some of this plant and hang it whole or put the chopped root into a cheese cloth and wrap it and hang it somewhere where it will dry. It protects against intrusion, so once it is dry hang it in your house or carry it in your car or on your person.

String Jar

This is probably one of the easiest protections to do. Get a clean jar with a lid, small ones work well for this. Whenever you find a stray thread or string you put it into the jar and put the lid back on. The thread can come from a piece of clothing, art project, random threads that show up from random place. I usually start mine with a few threads (you can cut some for this purpose) then I add to the jars as new strings are acquired. The idea is that anything that comes towards your home with ill intent will get caught in the threads and unable to find its way out. I tend to keep one by each door.

Floor Wash

This is a simple recipe to use on your floors after you mop.

- One quart distilled water
- A few drops of dish soap—the blue color is best as it adds extra protection.
- Three to five drops of your favorite protection oil

Begin by sweeping and mopping your floor as you normally would, then let it dry. Then, mop again with the mix above visualizing a protective blue light as you do so. Then, allow it to airdry. Repeat every few weeks or as needed.

Graveyard Dirt

Graveyard dirt is another versatile tool. But before you go grabbing your spade and jar, there is etiquette to follow when you go to the graveyard. Think of it like entering someone's house. You wouldn't just barge in and start taking their belongings and ordering them around. A graveyard is the home of the deceased who live there. Here's a little guide for collecting graveyard dirt.

What You Need

- Some pennies
- A hand trowel
- A jar with lid
- Flowers or other offering

When to Go

You will draw a lot less suspicion if you go buy some flowers and go visit during regular daylight hours. Someone walking in the cemetery at nighttime with a shovel in hand is likely to get the cops called on them. You don't want that. You've had enough of that.

How to Enter

You need to pay tithing to god/goddess/guardian of the cemetery. I keep a small jar of pennies in my car for this purpose. I take out a few, stop at the cemetery gate, say a few words, usually to the Greek goddess Hecate or the Roman Libitina, and toss a few near the entrance with my gratitude. While you are in the cemetery, be respectful. If you are going to hear a twig snap and go running out of the cemetery screaming, if you are going to vandalize, mock, or otherwise disrespect those who call it home, then you shouldn't even go.

Asking for Assistance

At this point you will want to ask, either mentally or out loud, who would be willing to help you. You will have to be paying attention to get your answer. This means having your phone put away, being relaxed (not rushed), and using all your clair- senses to "listen" for your answer. Some of you may find it easier to find a specific grave and ask them. Family members, police officers, firefighters, military members, and those who held similar occupations that are protective in nature, are usually good candidates. You will still want to ask their permission before you move on to the next step.

Collecting the Dirt

Some things to be cautious of when collecting dirt are the laws in your state and the respect you give to the grave. In some areas it is illegal to collect graveyard dirt. In others, you can with permission of the family, and still others, the laws depend on the type of the graveyard. Since my general attitude is to discourage you from participating in illegal activities, I'm going to give the ideal, then your alternative options.

Traditionally, you would dig a small hole about where their right hand or heart would be and put the dirt in the jar. You don't need tons of dirt. Just fill a small or medium jar. If you find that the dirt is particularly tough or get a feeling that maybe this isn't the one to collect dirt from, honor this and move on.

The alternative is to collect dirt from just outside the boundaries of the cemetery. You can also check with local shops to see if they carry it. Sometimes it is sold as a souvenir at touristy cemeteries. There is one more option: if you have access to the area where a beloved family pet has been buried, you can follow the process of collecting your dirt from here. Once you have collected the dirt, put on the lid and label it with the individuals name and the date you collected it. Leave your flowers or other offering in the hole and fill in the remainder with surrounding dirt. Say thank you to the deceased and spend a moment honoring them before leaving.

How to Use

At sundown, walk around your home and sprinkle the dirt around the perimeter. Say the following words "___Spirit's name___, I thank you for protecting this place, may your protection last throughout all time and space. Welcome." If you live in an apartment, you can put the cemetery dirt in a potted house plant and keep it near your door.

Wards

Warding is a way of protecting your home, your person, or another person by having an item serve as a ward or guardian for the space or person. I like to choose an item or statue that could have a living counterpart, for example, a dragon, tiger, a skull instead of a rock or button. Though this is not a steadfast rule.

Once you have selected your object, you will want to cleanse it physically and energetically. Then hold it in your hands, if it has eyes, look it in the eyes and name it. Say its name out loud. "___Name of being___, I put you here to guard and protect this home and all within it." Starting at the front door, walk the area you want protected while holding your ward. This may involve going outside, if so, do so. At every significant spot pause for a moment and say, "This land is yours to survey, guard it well and keep evil away." Make your way around the area you want protected until you are back at the front door.

Now, you will want to move your ward to their home. Pick an area they like, preferably with a view of the front door. Set them in their spot. To make sure that they have a permanent source of energy, you are going to give them roots going into the earth. This sounds complicated, but it isn't. You are going to see in your mind's eye a blue light forming in the center of your ward. Imagine this light growing roots and these roots going into the center of the earth. When you feel they are all the way there, bring your attention to the blue ball again. This time you are going to imagine branches going up into the sky and continuing into the universe. When these branches are to the point where the universe began, bring your attention back to the ward. Stand in front of it and say these words "__Name of being__, you are fed by sky and by earth. You are here now to protect this hearth. May you protect me and mine, until I release you or the end of time."

Now, you will want to anoint your ward with a few drops of oil. If you feel like this object has changed, it is because it has. You have given it life. It is no longer a thing, just some inanimate object. Because of this you will want to "feed" your ward periodically. You do this by lighting a tealight, anointed with some oil, close to your ward with the intention that it is being fed. Don't worry, after a while it will start letting you know when this needs to happen.

PROTECTIVE GODS

Do not be afraid to call upon the gods and goddesses. I think there is a tendency when one is new to any of the Pagan religions to carry in attitudes, feelings, perceptions, and beliefs from one's previous faith. I can't speak for everyone's experience, but I have never had any of the gods act as if I was bothering them when I came forward with a genuine need. I've had them tell me to calm down. I've had them tell me that there is a mundane solution. But when I have called on one for protection, I have always received it. It is likely you have had a god or goddess calling to you already, if not that's fine, at least one will. Either way, I encourage you to connect with any of the following gods and goddesses.

Greek (Roman Equivalent)

There is a Roman equivalent for almost every Greek god. However, you will find nuances that differentiate their stories. So, while Artemis and Diana are very similar, they do have differences in their energy you will want to take notice of.

> *Artemis (Diana):* Goddess of the hunt, she is protective of dogs, her sacred animal.

> *Apollo (Apollo):* God of healing, the sun, poetry, archery, and medicine. He is a good protector for children.

> *Hermes (Mercury):* Messenger to the gods, Hermes can also protect livestock and farm animals.

> *Hygieia (Salus):* She is the goddess of well-being and safety.

> *Hecate (Trivia):* Call on her to protect newborn babies and homes. She is also the guardian of crossroads, so her aid is helpful whenever you find yourself at life's crossroads (like parole).

Celtic

Try to not limit your impression of the Celtic people to just Ireland, Scotland, Britain, and Wales. The Celtic tribes at one point spanned from the island around the modern UK inland to Germany, Italy, Spain, Greece, and more.

> *Dagda:* He is the father figure of the Celtic people. Call on him if you need that protective, fatherly energy.

> *Cú Chulainn:* Though he is more of a demigod and hero than a deity, his heroic and protective energy can be tapped into whenever it is needed.

> *Danu:* She has that mother goddess protective energy to her. On another note, if you have never worked with a deity before, she is a good first choice as she tends to be quite welcoming and understanding.

> *Annea Clivana:* She is a protective goddess worshipped by the Celtic people who resided near Italy.

Norse

The Old Norse peoples interacted with more than just gods and goddesses; they had a whole supernatural world which existed all around them.

> *Dís (singular)/Dísir (plural):* These are female protective ancestral spirits that are usually linked to one bloodline or clan.

Eir: She is a goddess known for her healing abilities. Blue is her color. To implore her healing, a blue candle may be used.

Vör: This goddess is linked to women's intuition.[26] As such she may be called on to prevent you from entering dangerous situations.

Syn: She is the goddess of real and figurative locks and gates.[27]

Hlín: She is a protector. Her name literally means that.[28] She can help you escape enemies.

Thor: One of the most well-known of the Norse gods, his hammer Mjölnir is still worn by many as a protective symbol.

Egyptian

There are literally thousands of Egyptian gods and goddesses. I have chosen a few to list here but know that these represent only a small portion of the plethora of old Egyptian gods one could work with.

Horus: Horus is the falcon-headed god of protection. He is linked with the sun and its healing properties.

---

26. Sons of Vikings, "Forgotten Viking Goddesses," Sons of Vikings, March 15, 2021, https://sonsofvikings.com/blogs/history/forgotten-viking-goddesses.
27. Ibid.
28. Ibid.

Serket: As a goddess who is a guardian to women and children, she is helpful to build a rapport with and have in your corner.

Bast/Bastet: She is the goddess probably best known for her connection with cats, but she is also a guardian of hearth and home.

Ipy/Opet: One benefit that the goddess Ipy has is that she provides magical protection to those who evoke her.

Bes/Bisu: Though we don't hear as much about him as some of the other deities from Egypt, during his day, he was one of the most popular gods. Call on him to protect women, children, restore order, and fend off malignant energy.[29]

A WITCHES LADDER

I like the Witches ladder because they are crafty (pun intended). If you have kids, you can spend an hour or two making them together. They do not have to be for protection. You can make a Witches ladder for prosperity, longevity, to bring peace, for anything really. You just change the colors and feather colors to suit your intention.

29. Mark, Joshua J. "Egyptian Gods - the Complete List." World History Encyclopedia. World History Encyclopedia, July 28, 2021. https://www.worldhistory.org/article/885/egyptian-gods—the-complete-list/.

What You Need

- Three cords. You will want the whole thing to be about 36 inches long when you are done. I like to get my cords 38–39 inches to allow for the loss due to the braiding and knotting. Natural material is best but not required.
  - › One red
  - › One black
  - › One white
- Nine feathers, white or black are good colors to use for protection.
- A safety pin and something to attach it to. You will need this to hold the cords in place while you braid them.

What to Do

First, knot the ends of the three cords together, leave a small bit of cord at the end. Then, affix this knot to whatever you are using to hold them in place. In my younger days, we safety pinned string to the jeans we had on. This is simple and effective. Just don't poke yourself.

Start at the knot and braid the cords together, visualizing protection while you do so. Every three or so inches you will knot in one of your nine feathers and state what it is for. "First feather, you are protection." "Second feather, you are protection." If you are making a Witches ladder for another purpose, you will say what each feather is for. Maybe the first is protection and the second is security, for example.

When you are done knotting in all nine feathers, braid another few inches, then tie a knot at the end. It is okay if there is some cord length left over. Then bring the two ends together, like a

U-shape. The feathers should alternate and look like the rungs of a ladder. Hang it in the highest spot in your house.

THREE STAGE PROTECTION SPELL

This spell exists in three parts. Each part serves to reinforce the last. You'll start with physically cleansing your body, then your space. For the purposes of this spell, you can start with either part one or part two. If you like to clean, then bathe, that is completely up to you. By cleansing before getting into the "active" part of the spell, part three, you are creating a clean slate for your work to have full potency and effect.

What You Need:
Part One

- Shower supplies
- Charcoal soap
- Sachet: Sea salt, lavender, and rosemary

Part Two

- Sage or palo santo
- Lighter or matches
- Shell or small bowl to catch ashes

Part Three

- One black candle (any size, tapers work well)
- Carving tool
- Lighter
- High John the Conqueror Oil

Part One

Cleanse yourself. Wash as you normally would with charcoal soap. Take a bath or a shower and really devote some time to cleaning every inch of you. Don't forget between the toes, behind your ears, and all those other too often neglected places. Rinse well. The take your sachet and rub it gently over your body. Imagine any bad connections being removed from your body. The unwanted connections will run down the drain with the water. Compost the herbs in your sachet.

Part Two

Next, cleanse your home. Physical cleansing comes first. Sweep, mop, and straighten any areas that are dingy or cluttered. This is a good time to downsize and donate those objects you have been meaning to get rid of. The floors and windows could all get a nice wash in preparation for the energy cleaning that makes up the next step. There is a floor wash recipe given later in this chapter. Feel free to use the recipe in this part of your protection spell.

When you begin your spiritual cleansing star at your front doorway light your sage or palo santo and draw a pentagram across your doorway. Say with a commanding voice "Any and everything that would cause me harm, I banish now, forever be gone." Move around your house widdershins (counterclockwise), stopping at every doorway and window and repeat the words. You may have to keep relighting your sage/palo santo along the way, so keep your lighter/matches handy.

Once you have completely circled your home, you should be back at your front door. Repeat the steps above only this time, move deasil (clockwise) and say, "This space is surrounded and free from harm. This space is encased in the protection of the gods."

Part Three (Optional)

If you feel your person or home has been attacked by an individual, pull out a black candle and carve a pentagram on it. Write the name of the person, if known, below it. Anoint the candle with High John the Conqueror oil while saying "Our connection is now broken. Our ties are now unbound. Your energy is returned to thee as the candle burns down." While you do this part of the spell, try to not have any harmful feelings or malicious thoughts towards the individual. It is tempting to want them to hurt if they have caused you to hurt, but this spell is not meant to be vindictive and you will be held in much higher esteem by the gods if you approach this as a protective parting of ways, not tit-for-tat.

CHAPTER 9
DELVING DEEPER

Education is often underrated. Educating yourself in this world full of misinformation means not believing everything you hear, read, or think. It means acknowledging that you don't know everything. And, it means having a discerning mind about who to believe on important matters. Education doesn't always mean traditional education, though it can. From the day we are born until the day we die, life is a continuous process of learning. The truth is that the Pagan faiths usually come with a fair amount of research ... reading myths, watching videos, attending workshops. This is how we build these skills up over time. You never stop learning. No matter how good or adept you become, there is *always* more to learn. In this chapter, we are going to talk about the different types of education which can help improve your life, and in many cases, your connection to the gods.

TRADITIONAL EDUCATION
Maybe you have been thinking about furthering your education for a while. Maybe only recently. Or maybe you have never thought about it before this moment. Regardless of where you find yourself, there are a lot of fields that you can enter without going against the ethics and principles you carry. The educational topics

mentioned in this section are just a starting point to get you thinking about what you might want to study. You will also notice that some of the fields may have certificates, degrees, and trade schools as options. For the sake of space, I'm only listing them under one category. Just know that there are other options available. Something else to be aware of is that working in certain profession may be more challenging to enter if you have a criminal record. More challenging, but not impossible.

GED

This is the first step for a lot of people. Let's take the ability to get a job out of the equation. Getting a GED will increase your self-awareness, self-confidence, and your thinking power. It opens the door to more educational opportunities. Plus, it is a huge achievement.

Trade School

There are several trades that coincide well with Pagan beliefs. The solar and wind industries are growing just to name two. Working in these field will enable you to be part of an eco-friendly future.

College

Going to college is more flexible than ever. Not everyone needs to go to an Ivy League school. A great way to ease yourself into the collegiate realm is to start at a community college. These are great because you can take a lot of your core classes, English, science, math, what have you at a more affordable price. And most have flexible entry requirements. Then if you want, you can move on to a four-year college. You can also explore online schools. One advantage to going to school in person is that many campuses have Pagan groups. This is a great way to build community (see chapter 1). Regardless of if your interests lie in botany, culinary arts, integrative health care, writing, art, or anything in between, there is probably a college that will offer a course in it.

SPECIALTY PROGRAMS

Maybe traditional college isn't for you. That's fine. There are other options, many of which you may have never even thought about. But they exist. The length of time a course takes is going to depend on where you go and what you study. But the structure often makes them better options for those who don't want to commit several years to study.

Energy Healing

There are courses all over the country that offer energy healing as a field of study. Some use Reiki and a series of attunements, but not all. You may also find courses that offer instruction in laying on of hands, pranic healing, qigong, distance healing, biofield energy healing, therapeutic touch (TC), and more.

Traditional Chinese Medicine (TCM)

Probably the best-known form of TCM is acupuncture. But there is a lot more to it. There are also Chinese herbs, acupressure, moxibustion, cupping/scraping, nutrition, and tui na massage. TCM focuses on treating the whole body, not just parts of it.

Ayurveda

This is a series of healing methods that comes from India to promote whole body healing. Ayurvedic practitioners may use dietary changes, yoga, massage, oils, and medicines made from plant parts to help treat their patients.

Wellness Counseling

Helping people make healthier life choices takes good communication skills. Wellness training teaches you how to communicate wellness skills to patients looking to have an active role in their health.

Nutrition

Most people do not eat correctly. In the US, there are places called food deserts where fresh, real food are not available within a distance that makes them accessible. Outside of food deserts, it is difficult to find anything even modestly nutritious at convenience store. This matters because what we take into our bodies affects our physical, mental, and spiritual health. As a nutritionist you can help people develop dietary plans that work for them and reduce their risk of chronic disease.

Beekeeping

Maybe the hustle and buzz-le of a 9-to-5 job isn't for you. For some, having a plot of land, some animals, and raising crops is exactly what they need to feel at peace and connected to the earth. For those who don't own a large plot of land, a beehive could be the next best thing. You will want to have at least a yard to host your hive.

Web Design

Though web design might not be Pagan related on its own, it can be if you are designing for sites for organizations that are progressive. Such as those that fight for change, stand up for equity, are ecologically friendly, witchy, support religious equality, and other such brands. You could also say that since you're working on the web, that Greek Arachne would be approving of your work.

Leadership Skills

The world needs more people in leadership roles who understand why preservation is important and who view the cultures of others with respect. You may not see it right now while you are doing all you can to complete parole, but your history, your story puts you in a position to be able to guide others. Start learning how to lead now so when the times comes for you to step into such a role, you are ready.

MAGICAL EDUCATION

At some point on your spiritual journey there will come a time when you want to dig below the surface. Paganism, in its many forms, offers a real chance to delve into the darkness within and walk through it, greet it as a friend and ally, and find a strength you never knew you had. It is all well and good to wear crystals, drink herbal teas, and adorn yourself in magical jewelry, but these things are just the surface. If you let them, the gods can take you to a world most never get to see. It won't be easy, but it is worth it.

There are several paths you can take of self-discovery. Each has their pros and their cons. My experience has been that whatever I have needed on my path, be it a teacher, a video series, or a book that appeared out of nowhere, it has always been provided as long as I look. That is why one of the terms for people who are new to magic is called "seekers." You must seek the information. Here are the ways you can do that.

Family

Back when Pagan practices prevailed, which is not as long ago as one might think, the traditions and lore were passed down family lines. Women would teach their daughters and granddaughters how to weave, spin, sing up the weather, and use herbs and charms. Men would teach their sons and grandsons how to hunt, tan hides, and live off the land. There would have been some legends and herb lore for wound dressing taught too. These practices were handed down so long that the reason behind them was often lost. Some family lines still have strong magic flowing in their veins.

Coven/Kindred/Grove

Covens can be thought of as a magical family or working unit. People who are interested in learning Witchcraft will sometimes seek out a coven and learn from the high priest/ess of that group. Some covens are more open to outsiders and may even host public sabbats. Others are more secretive, and you must be invited to join. Covens can be a great way to learn. Do use a bit of common sense though. If you are attending ritual and are being "required" to do anything that makes you uncomfortable, leave. You don't want to learn from them anyway. The Heathen equivalent to a coven is Kindred and the Druid/Celtic equivalent is a Grove. The tend to have the same mix of open and invite only groups.

SIDE DISCIPLINES RELATED TO PAGANISM

A lot of Pagans will develop a particular affinity for a specific discipline and focus on that one area primarily. Having a niche can be advantageous. It may seem like there are so many topics that it would be impossible to ever cover them all in depth, that's because there are. Some topics are so vast you could spend a lifetime studying nothing else. Astrology is one such discipline. When you are figuring out what appeals to you dip your toes in the water, learn a little bit about the subjects that interest you. Then you can decide what you would like to dedicate more time to. This way you have a general knowledge base on which to build.

Astrology

This is more than just knowing your birth chart or reading you horoscope. Astrology includes planetary shifts that impact the whole of the human species. There are many great books on astrology available. Many metaphysical and occult shops will offer intro classes, check their website. If these don't work for you, there are also classes available online.

Divination

This is a broad category. In truth, you only need to be good at one or two types of divination. The rest can be fun to study, but while you are new, pick your favorite and try to learn it well before moving on to others. Check your local occult stores to see if they are offering classes in your preferred divination type. If not, look online. I usually bypass the ads that come up and start with the first unpaid listing and go from there.

Mythology

If you want to be an expert on mythology, read. There are great translations and interpretations available. If you don't have a big book budget, all you need is a library card. There are sometime free versions of classical books available in e-format too. Yes, some can be found online, but there are stories in Norse, Greek, and Celtic folklore that I have never seen on a website. I'm sure the same is true for other myths. Once you read them, investigate how they fit in the context of that culture. You can know so much about a group of people, and what they valued, from the stories they told.

Stones

Stones and gems have their own personality, their own energy. They might not be alive in the way we understand life, but they are far from being just random innate objects. Some stones, like lava rock, can form in twenty years.[30] Others, like amber, can take several million years to form. Rocks don't need to be a specific type to be powerful either. If you were, or have, a child who picks up rocks because they are a "nice rock," then you know this to be fact.

Spirituality

One of the most beautiful things about understanding your own spirituality is that you get pull pieces from wherever it feels right to do so. This "salad bar" approach means that if you want to apply Buddhist practices to your Pagan faith, you can as long as you honor and respect them. Some people will devote their whole lives to connecting with the Divine. This could lead to adventures living among the Saami people or attending Native American sweat lodges or seeing the sunrise at Stonehenge on the solstice. All these experiences have something unique and beautiful to offer. Just be open to them if they are offered.

PAGAN DEGREE SYSTEMS

Though not the case for all working groups, having levels of study to denote adeptness are common within Paganism. Even if you are a solitary practitioner, knowing these terms can help you follow your progress and understand what steps you want to take next. Three levels are common. In Wicca and Witchcraft, these

---

30. "Volcano Watch - How Do Lava Flows Cool and How Long Does It Take?" United States Geological Survey, February 28, 2019, https://www.usgs.gov /center-news/volcano-watch-how-do-lava-flows-cool-and-how-long-does-it -take.

will be the first, second, and third degrees. In the Order of Bards, Ovates, and Druids (OBOD) the three levels are Bard, Ovate, and Druid. Similar structures may appear in other groups as well.

Dedication

A dedication is something you can do on your own. It is meant to be a specific period of time that you dedicate to exploring Paganism, usually a year and a day. After this period, you can choose to keep going down your path or explore something else. In the three-level system, this is level "0." This is where if you are not sure if Paganism is right for you, you give yourself some time to find out. If, at the end of this time you find out that it's not for you, you may go with blessings. If you want to continue, you may renew your dedication for another year, three years, five years, or make it life-long. There is a self-dedication ritual at the end of this chapter that you may use and adapt for this purpose.

Initiation

Initiation isn't about how many books you've read or the number of sacred tattoos you have. It is about being in a certain stage in your spiritual evolution. For those of you working in a coven or church, there will specific guidelines that the high priestess and/ or high priest require to move on to the next degree. It is important to remember though, that while the high priest/ess may perform the ritual and serve as the conduit, the initiation comes from the gods. The guidelines listed for each are based off the training I received. When you see the term "study," this does not mean that you read a book over the course of a year, and you are done. This is a series of lessons that was studied over at least a year-and-a-day. For many, it takes longer, and that is okay. Do not be in such a rush to complete levels that you miss the lessons.

First Degree

The requirements include writing and hosting a sabbat ritual. This is held in front of others. The dedicant needs to have studied the course and materials provided for a *minimum* of a year and a day. And they need to make their own robe and cord to indicate their level of study.

Second Degree

To advance to a second degree, the initiate must have completed a first degree and have studied again for a *minimum* of a year-and-a-day. They need to write and host an esbat (full or new moon ritual), complete with all the components including a meditation and raising the cone of power. Part of achieving the second degree may also include the teaching of first-degree material to dedicants, and therefore prove that they are capable of teaching. The cord for second degree must also be made. And the groups Book of Shadows will have been hand copied by the initiate before being initiated to second degree.

Third Degree

This is the level at which, in most cases, a person may become a high priest or priestess. If you are in a coven that already has a member serving this role, you may be asked to fill in as an officiant when the high priest/priestess is not available or serve in other leadership type roles. It is common for a third degree initiate to facilitate classes for the first and second-degree initiates.

Teaching Others

If you want to teach others or take a program into jails or prisons, you need to get approval from the facility. Each state is a little different and state versus federal facilities will have different rules and hoops to jump through. The process can sometimes be redundant, but I can tell you that Pagan volunteers are so needed in prisons. If Alexandria Temple had not come to volunteer when I was incarcerated, my life might have taken a very different course.

The tricky part for a lot of people is knowing what to teach. In my first book, *Paganism for Prisoners*, I provide an outline of thirteen lessons that can serve as a starting point. Eventually I will be creating an online training course for this purpose. There are also some temples and schools which offer an initiation/degree type program. But what I would recommend is contacting temples and covens that already do ministry and seeing how they suggest getting involved. This was the path I followed. There was a temple that did Pagan ministry when I was incarcerated, and they provided my second-degree initiation (later my third) and vouched for my credentials.

GODS AND GODDESS OF WISDOM, EDUCATION, AND LEARNING

Hopefully, there is enough information in this section to give you some ideas of what you want to explore. Learning is a life-long process with the next step always right of you. The importance of education and learning can be found among the stories of the gods, goddesses, and other ethereal being that have survived through the ages. Whenever you feel stuck, like you don't know what to do next or if your educational path is the right one, you can call on them to guide you and give you strength. Now that you have some experience in Pagan practices, and hopefully meditation and spell work, you can call upon deities besides your patron. The acquisition of wisdom is a skill everyone should invest in. These deities can help you in your educational pursuits.

Athena: Greek. Goddess of wisdom.

Apollo: Greek. God of artistic and creative knowledge.

Hermes: Greek. God of cunning.

Minerva: Roman. Goddess of wisdom and crafts.

Neptune: Roman. God of the sea, keeper of the knowledge of water.

Odin: Norse. Gave his left eye for knowledge. He quests for knowledge and wisdom.

Mímir: Norse. Wisest of Æsir.

Kvasir: Norse. God of inspiration.

Frigg: Norse. Goddess who knows the future, but never tells.

Vör: Norse. Goddess of wisdom.

Saga: Norse. Goddess of wisdom.

Ecne: Celtic. Personification of wisdom.

Ogma: Celtic. Invented ogham writing system.

Thoth: Egyptian. Scribe. God of knowledge and wisdom.

Isis: Egyptian. Goddess of wisdom.

Anahit: Armenian. Goddess of wisdom.

Tir: Armenian. God of writing, wisdom, school, and the arts.

Enki: Sumerian. God of intelligence.

Nidaba: Sumerian. Goddess of learning and writing.

SPELL FOR INSIGHT

When faced with a dilemma or a quandary, it can be difficult to see the best solution, especially if you are close to the problem. This spell will help you to clear your head and let the universe provide you with answers you seek. Do this spell as soon as possible before bed. The idea is to reach a total and complete state of relaxation.

What You Need

- Bathtub or one good sized piece of clear quartz
- A strip of purple paper
- An amethyst crystal
- A pen

Preparation

The first thing you will want to do is take a bath in dim lighting. The water should be warm enough to be comfortable, but not too hot. If you do not have access to a bath, you may rub a clear quartz crystal all over your body while you sit in dim lighting. Get yourself ready for bed in your usual manner but be sure to put on your most comfortable pajamas.

Spell

On the piece of purple paper, write your problem as a question. For example, "Which job should I take?" Try to keep your question simple and singular. If you are writing five different questions, it will be hard to know which one is being answered.

Once your question has been written down, wrap the strip of paper around the amethyst while chanting the following:

> Hypnos, Greek god of sleep
> Answers to my question I do seek
> While I rest in slumber this night
> Bring the solution to my conscious mind.
> When I wake, the answer is clear
> May I follow it without anxiety or fear.

Place the wrapped amethyst in your pillowcase. As you head towards sleep, do your best to keep the question out of your mind. Trust that you will know what to do in the morning.

The next morning, the answer will be clear. Trust it. As an offering to Hypnos, take your amethyst to a place in nature, preferably by water, and bury it with thanks. Burn the strip a paper signaling that the problem is no longer a problem and that a solution has been found.

CONCLUSION

Here we are at the conclusion of the book, but this is just the beginning of your journey. I understand that parole is tough. There was a time when I believed that no one ever broke free from the cycle of incarceration, parole, recidivism, wash, rinse, repeat. I was wrong. Not only did I do it, but I also see others do it and go on to live amazing lives. This is my hope for you and the thought behind each chapter that lies within this book.

Time and time again I have wished that the lessons I learned, and the impact they had on me, could be passed on to you in one seamless bundle. But my lessons are just that, mine. Just as yours will be yours. It would be impossible for me to provide you with guidance for every single hardship, challenge, victory, or milestone you may encounter. Even if I could, I wouldn't, as it would take away some of the beauty of discovering these things for yourself.

What I will say is this. The woman I am today barely recognizes the girl I was many years ago. Life has unfolded in ways that are magical and raw and surprising. But it did not come from nothing. There are countless hours of work that have gotten me to this point … thousands of tears … weeks spent swallowing uncomfortable truths, and I am still far from done. I absolutely believe in the ability of every single one of you to step off the path that leads you back into a cell and onto one that leads to real life. Use these chapters as guide, build from them, reshape them, come up with creative ways to implement them and make them your own. In time you may find that you knew what you needed to do this whole time.

Blessings,

Awyn

RESOURCES

This list is just a starting point. A quick internet search can put you in touch with hundreds more. There is help for everything from substance abuse to depression to PTSD and so much in between. Asking for help is part of self-care and self-care should always be a priority.

Substance and Behavior Addiction

- Alcoholics Anonymous (AA), www.aa.org
- Narcotics Anonymous (NA), www.na.org
- Crystal Meth Anonymous (CMA), www.crystalmeth.org
- Cocaine Anonymous (CA), www.ca.org
- Co-Dependents Anonymous (CoDA), www.CoDA.org
- Advocates for Recovery (AFR), www.advocatesforrecovery.org
- Pagans in Recovery, https://www.facebook.com /groups/183170075056373
- Recovery Dharma, www.recoverydharma.org
- SMART Recovery, www.smartrecovery.org
- Gamblers Anonymous, www.gamblersanonymous.org/ga
- Overeaters Anonymous (OA), www.oa.org

Friends and Families

- Al-Anon, www.al-anon.org
- Nar-Anon, www.nar-anon.org

Mental Health Resources

- National Suicide Prevention Hotline: 1-800-273-8255 or text HELLO to 741741 or go to suicidepreventionlifeline .org
- Depression and Bipolar Support Alliance (DBSA): www .dbsalliance.org/crisis/suicide-hotline-helpline -information/
- The Blue Bench (sexual assault survivors): www .thebluebench.org
- RAINN (Sexual violence organization): www.rainn.org
- Help for Adult Victims of Child Abuse (HAVOCA): www.havoca.org
- Adult Survivors of Child Abuse (ASCA): www .ascasupport.org
- The WINGS Foundation (childhood sexual abuse support): www.wingsfound.org
- National Association of Adult Survivors of Child Abuse (NAASCA): www.naasca.org
- National Sexual Violence Resource Center (NSVRC): www.nsvrc.org
- PTSD Alliance: www.ptsdalliance.org
- PsychologyToday.com and SAMHSA.gov have additional resources for support groups of many different types. The Department of Veteran's Affairs has specific resources for PTSD

RECOMMENDED READING

Beinfield, Harriet, and Efrem Korngold. *Between Heaven and Earth: A Guide to Chinese Medicine.* New York: Ballantine Books, 1992.

Brennan, Barbara. *Hands of Light: A Guide to Healing Through the Human Energy Field.* New York: Bantam Books, 1988.

Cunningham, Scott. *The Complete Book of Incense, Oils, and Brews.* St. Paul, MN: Llewellyn Publications, 2002.

Hoffman, David. *The Herbal Handbook: A User's Guide to Medical Herbalism.* Fairfield, CT: Healing Arts Press, 1998.

Kaptchuk, Ted J. *The Web That Has No Weaver: Understanding Chinese Medicine.* New York: McGraw-Hill, 2008.

Kowalchik, Claire, William H. Hylton, and Anna Carr. *Rodale's Illustrated Encyclopedia of Herbs.* Emmaus, PA: Rodale Press, 1998.

Murray, Michael T. *The Healing Power of Herbs: The Enlightened Person's Guide to the Wonders of Medicinal Plants.* New York: Gramercy Books, 2004.

Oschman, James L. "Chapter 17. Energy Medicine in Daily Life." In *Energy Medicine: The Scientific Basis*, 2nd ed., 297–330. Edinburgh: Elsevier, 2016.

Sapolsky, Robert. *Why Zebras Don't Get Ulcers: The Acclaimed Guide to Stress, Stress-Related Diseases, and Coping.* New York: Holt Paperbacks, 2004.

Starhawk. *The Spiral Dance: A Rebirth of the Ancient Religion of the Great Goddess*. New York: HarperCollins Publishers, 1979, 1999.

Zukav, Gary. *The Dancing Wu Li Masters*. New York: William Morrow and Company, 1979.

BIBLIOGRAPHY

"A Brief History of Chalice Well." Chalice Well Trust. Accessed August 19, 2022. https://www.chalicewell.org.uk /our-history/a-brief-history-of-chalice-well/.

Akers, Michael, and Grover Porter. "What Is Emotional Intelligence (EQ)?" PsychCentral. Accessed July 30, 2020. https://psychcentral.com/lib/what-is-emotional-intelligence-eq/.

Badnjarevic, Dejan. "15 Major Celtic Gods and Goddesses (You Need to Know About)." The Irish Road Trip. Accessed January 12, 2021. https://www.theirishroadtrip.com /celtic-gods-and-goddesses/.

BBC Staff. "Earliest Music Instruments Found." *BBC News*, May 25, 2012. https://www.bbc.com/news /science-environment-18196349.

Bertone, Holly J. "Which Type of Meditation Is Right for You?" Healthline. Accessed October 2, 2020. https://www.healthline .com/health/mental-health/types-of-meditation.

Bullock, B. Grace. "What Focusing on the Breath Does to Your Brain," *Greater Good Magazine*, October 31, 2019. https://greatergood.berkeley.edu/article/item/what_focusing_on _the_breath_does_to_your_brain.

CDC staff. "CDC Washington Testimony July 11, 2019." Centers for Disease Control and Prevention. Last updated July 12, 2019.

https://www.cdc.gov/washington/testimony/2019
/t20190711.htm.

Cunningham, Scott. *Wicca, Living Wicca, The Complete Book of Incense, Oils & Brews*. New York: One Spirit, 2003.

"Emotional Intelligence in Leadership: Learning How to Be More Aware." MindTools. Accessed September 5, 2021. https://www.mindtools.com/pages/article/newLDR_45.htm.

Encyclopaedia Britannica Online. "Mercury." Accessed May 21, 2021. https://www.britannica.com
/topic/Mercury-Roman-god.

Encyclopædia Britannica Online. "Yggdrasill." Accessed May 29, 2021. https://www.britannica.com/topic/Yggdrasill.

Featherstone, Alan Watson, Edward Baker, Paul Kendall, Shirley Pottie, and Dan Puplett. "Rowan Tree Mythology and Folklore." Trees for Life. Accessed March 5, 2021. https://treesfor-life.org.uk/into-the-forest/trees-plants-animals/trees/rowan/rowan-mythology-and-folklore/.

"Forgotten Viking Goddesses." Sons of Vikings. Accessed March 15, 2021. https://sonsofvikings.com/blogs/history/forgotten-viking-goddesses.

Gaia Herbs. "Herbs to Help Support a Healthy and Happy Heart." Gaia Herbs. Last updated 2021. https://www.gaiaherbs.com/blogs/seeds-of-knowledge/herbs-to-help-support-a-healthy-and-happy-heart.

Greenfield, Mike. "Knight's Honour Code of Chivalry." Widjiitiwin. Last updated September 8, 2017. https://widjiitiwin.ca/knights-honour-code-of-chivalry/.

"The Growing Crisis of Chronic Disease in the United States." Partnership to Fight Chronic Disease. Accessed 2020. https://www.fightchronicdisease.org/sites/default/files/docs/GrowingCrisisofChronicDiseaseintheUSfactsheet_81009.pdf.

Hadhazy, Adam. "Think Twice: How the Gut's 'Second Brain' Influences Mood and Well-Being." *Scientific American*, February 12, 2010. https://www.scientificamerican.com/article/gut-second-brain/.

Hall, Judy. *The Crystal Bible: the Definitive Guide to Crystals and Their Use*. London: Godsfield, 2009.

"Healing by Touch." Encyclopedia of Occultism and Parapsychology. Encyclopedia.com. Accessed March 3, 2021. https://www.encyclopedia.com/science/encyclopedias-almanacs-transcripts-and-maps/healing-touch.

Hoffman, David. *The Herbal Handbook: A User's Guide to Medical Herbalism*. Rochester, VT: Healing Arts Press, 1998.

"Homeopathy." National Center for Complementary and Integrative Health, U.S. Department of Health and Human Services. Last updated July 2018. https://www.nccih.nih.gov/health/homeopathy.

Huson, Paul. *Mastering Herbalism: A Practical Guide*. New York: Stein and Day, 1975.

Jones, Andrew Zimmerman. "How Quantum Physics Explains the Invisible Universe." ThoughtCo. Last updated August 16, 2019. https://www.thoughtco.com/quantum-physics-overview-2699370.

Jones, Andrew Zimmerman. "Newton and Einstein's Major Laws of Physics Help Explain the Universe." ThoughtCo. Last updated July 3, 2019. https://www.thoughtco.com/major-laws-of-physics-2699071.

"Juturna" Encyclopedia Mythica. Last updated March 3, 1997. https://pantheon.org/articles/j/juturna.html.

Kaptchuk, Ted J. *The Web That Has No Weaver: Understanding Chinese Medicine*. New York: McGraw-Hill, 2008.

King, L.W., trans. "The Code of Hammurabi." The Avalon Project: Code of Hammurabi, Yale Law School. Last updated 2008. https://avalon.law.yale.edu/ancient/hamframe.asp.

Kowalchik, Claire, William H. Hylton, and Anna Carr. *Rodale's Illustrated Encyclopedia of Herbs*. Emmaus, PA: Rodale Press, 1998.

Lindberg, Sara. "Brain Exercises: 13 Ways to Boost Memory, Focus, and Mental Skills." Healthline. Last updated August 7, 2019. https://www.healthline.com/health/mental-health/brain-exercises.

Mark, Joshua J. "Egyptian Gods: The Complete List." World History Encyclopedia. Accessed July 28, 2021. https://www.worldhistory.org/article/885/egyptian-gods—the-complete-list/.

Mckenzie, Dan. "Some Healing Wells and Waters, with a Suggestion as to the Origin of the Votive Offering." *Proceedings of the Royal Society of Medicine* 7 (1914): 177–92. https://doi.org/10.1177/003591571400701611.

Milanowski, Ann. "Don't Eat Until You're Full—Instead, Mind Your Hara Hachi Bu Point." Health Essentials from Cleveland Clinic. Last updated September 4, 2020. https://health.clevelandclinic.org/dont-eat-until-youre-full-instead-mind-your-hara-hachi-bu-point/.

Murray, Michael T. *The Healing Power of Herbs: The Enlightened Person's Guide to the Wonders of Medicinal Plants*. New York: Gramercy Books, 2004.

Oschman, James L. "Chapter 17. Energy Medicine in Daily Life." In *Energy Medicine: The Scientific Basis*, 2nd ed., 297–330. Edinburgh: Elsevier, 2016.

Olson, Eric J. "How Many Hours of Sleep Do You Need?" Mayo Foundation for Medical Education and Research. Last updated

June 6, 2019. https://www.mayoclinic.org /healthy-lifestyle/adult-health/expert-answers /how-many-hours-of-sleep-are-enough/faq-20057898.

Pagán, Camille Noe, and Nayana Ambardekar. "Aromatherapy and Essential Oils for Relaxation and Stress Relief." WebMD. Accessed January 23, 2020. https://www.webmd.com /balance/stress-management/aromatherapy-overview#1.

Park, Kyungho. "Role of Micronutrients in Skin Health and Function." The Korean Society of Applied Pharmacology. Last updated May 2015. https://www.ncbi.nlm.nih.gov /pmc/articles/PMC4428712/.

Prakash, M., and J. Carlton Johnny. "Things You Don't Learn in Medical School: Caduceus." *Journal of Pharmacy and Bioallied Sciences 7* (April 2015): S49–S50. https://www.ncbi.nlm.nih .gov/pmc/articles/PMC4439707/.

"Precious Metals and Other Important Minerals for Health." Harvard Health. Last updated July 2018. https://www.health .harvard.edu/staying-healthy/precious-metals-and -other-important-minerals-for-health.

Rand, William Lee. *Reiki: The Healing Touch, First and Second Degree Manual.* New Delhi, India: Health Harmony, 2014. https://www.reiki.org/faqs/what-history-reiki.

"Religion 101: Ancestor Worship in Ancient Europe and the Arctic." Daily Kos. Last updated April 10, 2019. https://www .dailykos.com/stories/2019/4/3/1847528/-Religion-101 -Ancestor-Worship-in-Ancient-Europe-and-the-Arctic.

Reynolds, Bob. "In Every Land and Time: An Informal History of Hands-on Healing." LifeSpark Cancer Resource. Last updated August 28, 2018. https://www.lifesparknow.org /every-land-time-informal-history-hands-healing/.

Sawyer, Wendy, and Peter Wagner. "Mass Incarceration: The
    Whole Pie 2020." Prison Policy Initiative. Last updated March
    24, 2020. https://www.prisonpolicy.org/reports/pie2020.html.
Smith, Henry Preserved. "The Laying-on of Hands." *The American
    Journal of Theology* 17, no. 1 (1913): 47–62. Accessed March 3, 2021.
    http://www.jstor.org/stable/3154793.
Toolkit, London, ed. "Glastonbury Chalice Well, White Spring
    & Wearyall Hill." Visiting Glastonbury Chalice Well, White
    Spring & Wearyall Hill. Accessed May 28, 2021. https://www
    .londontoolkit.com/whattodo/glastonbury_chalice_well.htm.
"Volcano Watch: How Do Lava Flows Cool and How Long Does
    It Take?"United State Geological Survey. Last updated February
    28, 2019. https://www.usgs.gov/center-news/volcano-watch
    -how-do-lava-flows-cool-and-how-long-does-it-take.
Wesselman, Hank. "3 Causes of Spiritual Illness." Omega.
    Accessed January 22, 2021. https://www.eomega.org
    /article/3-causes-of-spiritual-illness.
Wm, Kowalchik Clare and Hylton. *Rodale's Illus. Encyclopedia of
    Herbs*. Emmaus, PA: Rodale Press, 1987.

INDEX

A

TO WRITE TO THE AUTHOR

If you wish to contact the author or would like more information about this book, please write to the author in care of Llewellyn Worldwide Ltd. and we will forward your request. Both the author and publisher appreciate hearing from you and learning of your enjoyment of this book and how it has helped you. Llewellyn Worldwide Ltd. cannot guarantee that every letter written to the author can be answered, but all will be forwarded. Please write to:

Awyn Dawn
℅ Llewellyn Worldwide
2143 Wooddale Drive
Woodbury, MN 55125-2989

Please enclose a self-addressed stamped envelope for reply,
or $1.00 to cover costs. If outside the U.S.A., enclose
an international postal reply coupon.

Many of Llewellyn's authors have websites with additional information and resources. For more information, please visit our website at http://www.llewellyn.com